My Mother
the story of a courageous woman

Helmut Lemke

authorHOUSE®

AuthorHouse™
1663 Liberty Drive
Bloomington, IN 47403
www.authorhouse.com
Phone: 833-262-8899

Published by AuthorHouse 07/17/2020

ISBN: 978-1-7283-6712-5 (sc)
ISBN: 978-1-7283-6713-2 (e)

Print information available on the last page.

To my Children and their spouses	Michael
	Krista
	Hanno
My Grandchildren	Madison
	Tobin
	Justin
	Tomas

To Relatives and Friends who have known and valued my mother and want to learn to know more about her.

Wiehlerchronik 2000, editor and co-author   2000
history of my Mother's family

Lemke Chronik   2002
History of my Father's family

Crossing Frontiers   2007
Autobiography

A Life Fully Lived (Loving Hildegard)   2010
The story of an immigrant family

Mennonite Artists' Home, co-author   2010

Über Grenzen Hinaus   2014
Autobiography, German edition

Slipping the Noose   2018
Two escape stories

Contents

Chapter one
Childhood

Mothers have a special place in the family. They are the life-givers, not only of the physical but often also of the social and spiritual life of the family.

Selma Lemke, my mother, or Tante Selma, as she was usually known by friends and relatives, was such a live-giver. She was a marvellous, remarkable, unforgettable woman.

She was born in a small village in West Prussia, Germany, in eighteen hundred ninety six. Her father, Johann Wiehler, the sixth of ten children of a Mennonite family, had bought a farm in a small remote settlement, Sparau, off the village of Preußisch Königsdorf and became a very successful and proficient farmer.

As a young man he was said to have lived a somewhat loose life, he was popular in the bar and got into trouble. A friend took him once to a Christian revival meeting and that changed his life. He saw what alcohol can do to people. He joined the Blue Cross organisation and never drank a drop of alcohol again. He turned into a good husband and father.

Opa Wiehler was a patriarch who represented his family in public, cared and provided for it and felt responsible for it.

Mother's parents

Oma Wiehler was a quiet woman. She was struck with an age-related macular degeneration and had turned almost blind. In her younger years she was known to be an energetic, efficient housewife. Through her handicap she had become a somewhat withdrawn person. She was a sensitive woman. When we came into her room she would recognise us by our steps; on my arrival, hearing me come in, she would call my name as a question, Helmut? and most of the time she was right. Then she would ask what I was up to. Otherwise she was not engaging us much. When we visited our grandparents my mother would remind me, honour your grandmother, greet her kindly with a kiss. As a young boy I was not too fond of kissing her wrinkled face.

Grandfather honoured his wife and supported her

graciously. The two complemented each other. On a sunny day they would sit under the big linden tree in front of their house. Grandfather would read to her aloud, usually from the Bible, and she would listen. When someone was approaching she was aware by the sound and would ask: Johann, who is coming? Grandfather was hard of hearing and had not noticed anything.

Farmers in these remote, lonely areas, away from the village, had a tendency to seek company with their neighbours in a bar and spend the earnings from their farms on alcohol. This sometimes cost them their farm and they went bankrupt and their wives did not have enough money to feed their family. Opa Wiehler tried to counsel them and if that showed no results, bought their farms, used the land and let them live in their houses. He would even offer them to work for him, so that they were able to support their families. Buying up several small farms increased the value of his property.

So my mother was born into a well-to-do family. Farmer couples at that time often had large families. They needed helping hands to run the farm. In mother's birth family were twelve children. Four died at childbirth or shortly after, seven lived into adulthood. In addition to his own dozen children, father adopted five orphan children.

There is one story I remember about my grandfather that impressed me immensely. When he already lived in his smaller farm in Pr. Rosengart, he would occasionally go back to his old homestead to see how his son managed it. I loved to go with him looking forward to playing with my cousins. I might have been eight years old. We started from church taking the shortcut across Epp's meadows. First grandfather would help me to jump over the drainage ditch from the trail on to the meadow on which the big herd of cows was peacefully grazing. I looked out for the bull and sure there he came running towards us. He stopped a few feet from us bellowing fiercely and digging up the grass with his hooves, his head down and his spiky horns pointing at us. I was scared stiff and hid behind my grandfather who kept on walking. He walked normally on, telling the bull to calm down, we would not do any harm to him. The bull was following us still bellowing but gradually a little softer, until we crawled through the fence on the other side of the meadow and then walked across the narrow wooden footbridge over the Thiene River on to his former farm. I admired my grandfather, his fearlessness. I wondered did he gain his strength from his trust in God or are older people not so fearful anymore.

My mother grew up in a carefree, protected environment; this gave her a feeling of security and self-confidence. Growing up in a large family taught her also some survival techniques, patience, sharing and waiting for her turn, good character traits which guided her through all her life. As little girls, she told me, she was walking with her favoured sister, Anna, along the banks of the small river near their house, fantasizing how they would explore the world when they grew up and where they would end up eventually.

In the family picture she is the one in the top row right and her sister Anna below her.

Mother's birth family, mother top right

Her father was a practical, conservative man. All his children helped on the farm and he taught them good work habits. He wanted his girls to become responsible housewives and mothers and the boys good farmers or tradesmen.

Mother and all her siblings attended public school. Getting to school required some energy. They lived about four km away from the village where the school was located, a forty minute walk each day. If the dirt road to the village was too muddy or the snow too high, they were allowed to ride to school. They did this for eight years.

My mother was not a very academically inclined student, but she was joyful and diligent and became the darling of teacher Schulz. After graduation from public school, the girls were sent to a home economics school and after graduation completed a practice year in a reputable household, to be able to apply what they had learned in school. The boys would attend the well known agriculture school. None of the children went to high school or university. Mother followed that pattern and attended the home economics school in the city after her public school graduation.

Her father had heard about the countess of Lagow, who was known for grooming girls and young women for aquiring good housekeeping and family management skills. He wrote to her and asked if she would accept his daughter and show her how to lead a Christian household and family. When he received a positive answer, my mother moved to Schloss Lagow and was 'adopted' for a year in the von Lagow family to observe and learn the art of creating a beautiful home for a Christian family.

In the kitchen the chef taught her how to prepare delicious meals, use spices to give food a different flavour and how to set a beautiful table. Frau von Lagow, a very gracious lady, taught her how to bring up children, to try to understand them with their different needs. She gave her a short, practical lesson in child psychology, how to talk to children at their different stages of growing up, teach them discipline with love and compassion and how to create an environment where everyone would feel accepted and valued. She also taught her how to invite guests courteously and entertain them graciously. All this was a valuable enrichment and refinement to what mother had observed from her parents at home.

CHAPTER TWO
MOTHER'S FAMILY

Each of mother's siblings found their own way. One after the other moved out from home. Elise, the oldest one, married a farmer and settled in a remote village in East Prussia. Helene and Anna were trained to become deaconesses, in an order which could be compared to an order for protestant nuns. I remember them dressed in their somewhat formal, long black habit with a white head covering. Helene later managed an old folks home, the *Lindenhaus*, which her father had established and Anna was matron of an orphanage in *Sorgenfrei* (care free) which he also supported. Connected with the orphanage was a small farm, which she, a farmer's daughter, could easily operate. The farm provided most of the basic food for the residents of the home. It also gave the children an opportunity to learn to take on some responsibilities and to have something to do, have some entertainment. Mother encouraged us and we loved to visit Tante Annchen in Sorgenfrei. Her place was beside a small river and we could go swimming, paddle and race in their canoes. Her house was always open. She was a warm and efficient matron.

Another example of Johann Wiehler's generosity: he bought a large farmhouse beside our Mennonite church, which he donated to *Friedenshort*, (place of peace) the same organisation to which mother's two sisters belonged. They converted it to an orphanage, the '*Tannenhaus*' and deaconess sister Margarete, in her black habit and white bonnet, became its matron.

Mother's father was frugal, almost stingy with himself and his family; his motto was: 'Simple living is godly' but he was very generous helping others and especially if it was done for 'the kingdom of God'.

When mother came back from Schloss Lagow, ready to apply what she had learned in practice, she fell in love with Ewald, a dashing young man. He was drafted into the army to fight in the First World War. She was looking forward for his return to get married and then received the sad news that he was killed on the western front. That was a hard blow for her.

Opa Wiehler founded, together with Adolf Lemke, a blacksmith-master from the neighbouring village, a Christian non-denominational fellowship, the *'Landeskirchliche Gemeinschhaft'*. On Sunday mornings Opa Wiehler went to the service in his Mennonite church and Opa Lemke to his Protestant church and in the evening both families and attendees from surrounding villages met in their fellowship for another more intimate, pious service and usually on Wednesday evenings they had a common Bible study. Both founders preached occasionally for the evening service.

Two stories go around about Johann Wiehler. One Wednesday evening, he had lead the Bible study and was driving home alone. He was tired from a full day of hard work and fell asleep in his seat on the wagon. The horses knew the way home and went through the open gate beside the house right unto the meadow. When he woke up in the morning he saw his horses grazing in the meadow and pulling the wagon behind them. He was surprised to find himself in the middle of a meadow instead of his warm bed.

The other story apparently happened in the middle of winter. He and his wife had driven to the evening service in an open sleigh. He sat in front and his wife in a seat behind him. On the way home the horses took the sharp curve from the village to the narrow dirt road leading to his house too quickly. He felt a slight jerk but did not think much about it. When he arrived home and intended to untie the horses he noticed his wife was not in the sleigh. That explained that jerk he thought. He drove back and found her in that curve lying in the snow in her fur coat. Now they arrived together at their home. I am not sure how much credence I can give these stories, but with this Grandfather it could have happened.

In his later years he used to fast every Monday for breakfast and lunch and spend the time praying and interceding for others. He prayed aloud and often had his window open like Daniel in the Old Testament.

He knew the miller Perschon. He brought his wheat and grain to his mill and the miller ground it for flour and grain for his animals. The miller was an alcoholic and abused his family. Grandfather was concerned about him. One early morning miller Perschon came to his house to ask for an advance payment. When he passed under his open window, he heard Johann Wiehler praying for him, that he would change his life, care better for his family and that God would free him from his alcoholism.

Hearing that hit him. Miller Perschon turned around, went home and never got drunk again.

Mother observed her father being an intercessor and a man of prayer, which left an impression on her and she followed his example.

The Landeskirchliche Gemeinschaft enlivened its services often with choir music and orchestral performances. Franz Lemke, Adolf Lemke's son, was the choirmaster and the conductor of a small string orchestra. He had taught the girls from the Wiehler and Lemke families to play guitars and join the orchestra. He also led the young peoples' group.

The fellowship was a place where young Christian people met, interacted and got acquainted with each other and often found their life partners there. So it happened that Franz learned to know Selma more intimately and found her attractive and she had qualities that he liked in a partner. They got married. Selma had by that time gotten over the loss of her former boyfriend who had died in the war.

Mother and Father

The aging Opa Wiehler had at this time transferred his estate in Sparau to his oldest son, Richard, and had bought a smaller farm in a village closer to the church. His youngest son, Heinrich, took over the main work on the farm and Helene left her order, exchanged her habit for a common dress and cared for her parents since her mother had turned almost blind. Tante Lenchen, as she was known, was the soul of this home, very generous and kind. Beggars passed on the news to each other: when you are hungry go there at noontime, you will be for sure invited for lunch.

Friends and relatives had coined their place '*Die grüne Aue*' (The green pasture) We children loved to visit the Grüne Aue. Tante Lenchen had always something special for us and she was a fantastic storyteller.

Opa Wiehler had a heart for the underprivileged. He tried to narrow the gap between rich and poor. Occasionally he would load a sack of flour, potatoes, vegetables and small packages of meat on his wagon and drive through the back lane where the poor, addicted and handicapped lived. The women in that area knew him already. When they saw his wagon approaching they came out of their houses with their bowls, handed them to him and he would fill them. He would also counsel the men who were addicted to alcohol and were negligent and abusive to their families.

Opa Wiehler liked to take us children along to show us life on the other side of the road. He wanted people to have a happy and decent life and believed if they knew the word of God and followed the teachings of Jesus, they could achieve that, so when it was appropriate he would spread the good news. He took the opportunity, when we were with him, to ask us to distribute Christian tracts to the homes in the neighbourhood. We did that because we thought that was important to him and we loved him but one part of this service we did not like. Some of the farms had vicious dogs which came barking to the gate, when we came close to the house. They scared us and we just stuck the tract into the fence and ran away.

Mother observed her father's Christian charitable activities and his concern for 'bringing the kingdom of God to earth', and followed his example in her own way throughout her life.

Chapter three
Raising a family

My parents, the newly married couple, bought a small farm not far from the Grüne Aue. Mother put into practice now what she had learned, how to establish a good household and make a cozy home for a young family.

As it was common at that time, young couples started to have a family shortly after they got married. So a little over a year after they had given their vows, Magdalena was born, two years later the second daughter Christa and finally a son Helmut. All three were strong, healthy babies.

At that time children were not delivered in a hospital, with a doctor present. A midwife would help to assist the woman with the birth of her baby at home. Strangely enough, the midwife that helped mother, was the wife of the village butcher.

Lemke family 1928

Magdalena had inherited more of the entrepreneurship of her father while Christa more the positive attitude, friendliness and helpfulness of her mother. When she was drafted to the Arbeitsdienst, the other girls would sometimes come to her for advice. When she came home on furlough she would ask her mother how to respond to questions of her fellow workers in regards to morality, sexuality and religion.

The farm of my parents was a multifaceted enterprise. Beside ploughing fields, mowing meadows and raising cattle, mother had planted a large vegetable garden, which would provide food, vegetables, different types of berries and herbs for the kitchen. She had allotted a small garden plot for each of us children, showed us how to prepare it, cultivate it and harvest what we had sown. I remember her telling us to go into the garden, pull out some carrots or radishes, wash them and eat them raw, they are good for you, they keep you healthy. Her concern was to put healthy and tasty food on the table for the wellbeing of her family.

We also had a large orchard with a variety of fruit trees. Beside the house grew an old big pear tree, higher than the house. I liked to climb high up to the top and hide in it.

The children in the village knew when the pears were ripe. They then snuck up to the farm, hoping to see father around somewhere. Father knew what they wanted. He would get his long pole with the bend wire loop on top, hook it over one of the high branches and pull hard that the pears tumbled down and the children were allowed to fill their baskets. Father was generous.

When we were old enough to help with work in the fields, mother would work beside us. She would patiently show us the difference between a weed, which had to be pulled out, and a useful plant, which had to be handled carefully. She made us aware of nature regenerating and preserving itself. We laid potatoes in the ground, covered them with earth and saw them come up months later again as full green plants, and in fall when we dug them up, the one potato had multiplied to a dozen or more.

Lemke family 1933

My parents were quite different in temperament. My mother, a short, well built person with bright shiny eyes, was an extrovert, an outgoing person, unpretentious but with a healthy self-esteem, who knew what she wanted and did it. She was helpful and made friends easily. She had a rich imagination and followed that up with actions. She had also an unusual intuition, which made her aware of difficult situations and may even have saved her life in dangerous circumstances.

I remember one little event. Mother took her bicycle to the field, parked it at the end of the driveway and walked into the meadow to look for the cows. When she came back she noticed that she had a flat tire, somebody had screwed out the valve. That had happened twice. On one of the following days she saw the neighbour kids, who were occasionally using our driveway as a shortcut to get home, going by. She stopped them and told one of the boys in a firm voice: Rudolf you took the valve out of my bicycle tire the other day, could you give it back to me please? Rudolf was stunned, how did she know? He could not deny it, put his had into his pocket and pulled out the valve. And give me the other one too, she told him and he pulled out the other valve. Mother told him in kind but firm words that it was not right to steal other people's property. She had no idea that Rudolf had done that.

My mother was a very practical, common sense person with a positive, friendly attitude.

My father, a tall, good-looking man, was an introvert, modest and somewhat withdrawn. It was not easy to learn to know him closely. Honesty and responsibility where some of his outstanding characteristics, which earned him high respect but did not make him popular. He was an artist at heart, very musical, he played several instruments: as soldier, the trumpet in the army's music corps, in his orchestra he played the leading violin or lute.

He could draw quite well. We had several small sketchbooks of his from the war, where he had recorded realistically the terrors of war, experiences with comrades, retreats, battles, prisoners and care of wounded soldiers.

At home he was a many-sided handyman, quite creative doing small repairs on the house and farm, building furniture and many of our toys came from his hand. I thought there was nothing he could not do. I still see the elaborate doll house with all the interiors he had built for the girls, painted in fresh, coordinated colours. Every Christmas a new toy or an old one newly decorated was on the gift table. Once he had carved a hobbyhorse with headgear and stirrups, which I could ride. The next year there stood a farmhouse with inventory, wagons, horses and cows, for me. His work had to be perfect before he let it out of his hands. Everything was a piece of art. One thing I missed in my father, I do not remember that he took me aside and showed me how to carve or build things. I could watch him and he would answer questions. I was often too shy to ask. He was very protective of his tools. They had to be clean and sharp. I remember I had secretly 'borrowed' some of his tools to carve a sailboat and had not put them back properly. When he found that out, I had to repeat ten times "I shall always put things back to the place from where I had taken them."

Father was not a passionate farmer like my mother's brothers. He had just married a farmer's daughter. I think his aptitude was more suited for that of an engineer and designer. He was humble by nature. His self-esteem was not very high. When the mayor of our village planned to retire, he suggested my father to replace him as mayor; he thought he would be well suited for that position, but father did not accept it. He said: I will do what I can do best for the community, be the First Aid man in the region. He had been a medic in the army.

My parents went through hard times shortly after their marriage. The results of the Versailles peace treaty that ended the First World War were quite devastating for the economy. They were unjust and revengeful. Germany had to accept the accusation of being responsible for the war, which was not true and had therefore to pay high reparation costs to the allied forces, especially France. That ruined many people's lives. Taxes were high and work was scarce. Farmers got very little for their farm products, barely enough to keep the farm going and many who had to make payments for their farm or equipment fell behind with paying their debts and had to declare bankruptcy. Many children went to bed hungry. Mother had an advantage, she could feed her children. Being farmers, we grew most of our basic food ourselves and could survive. We did butcher our own animals and had meat to eat. Hide and fur we could use for warm clothing.

Schlachtfest, butcher-day, was always a special event. Father had organised a team of workers. He would bring in the pig from the pigpen to the barn. Our next-door neighbour had been asked to come over and was now waiting inside to do his job. He was the anaesthetist. A little farther over sat Onkel Heinrich, mother's younger brother, with a butcher knife and sharpening stone beside him and in the kitchen ruled mother, waiting for the cut-up pig pieces to be brought in and was ready to process them. When father had the pig quieted down in the barn, the neighbour would swing the big sledgehammer and land it directly on the pigs forehead, that caused it to slump down. Onkel Heinrich would draw his knife to cut the unconscious pig's throat and let the blood flow out until the pig was dead. Now father would take over. Father never killed the animal himself. He always invited someone else to do the killing.

I was excited to watch the butchering procedure but father did not allow me to see the killing of the animal. Father and Onkel Heinrich would then lay the dead pig into the *Brühtrog*, a two-meter by one-meter watertight wooden box. Mother had boiling water ready and poured it over the pig to loosen its bristles. I could participate in the operation by shaving the bristles off its skin. Father would tie ropes on the hind legs of the pig and lift it up to eye height on one of the barn beams. Now came the most exciting part for me. Father would cut its belly open, show me the inside and give me a short lesson in anatomy. He pointed out where the heart was, what lung, kidney and stomach looked like and what the winding intestines were for. He cut those parts out very carefully and put them in a bowl. I took the bowl into the kitchen where mother had water boiling in the big kettle. She processed the parts further, cleaned out the intestines very thoroughly with a vinegar solution, filled them with ground meat and cut them to size to make meat sausage, liver sausage or blood sausages and cut up the ham to be hung in the smoke chamber. We later brought a package of meat to the neighbour as a thank you gift for his help.

My parents had made an agreement with the old couple from whom they had bought the farm that they would pay them a monthly amount as a pension as long as they lived, so payment could somehow be adjusted. My parents were very resourceful. Mother was a good seamstress and could alter, cut and re-sew old clothing and make it fit for pants or jackets for us children. She could regain threads from a worn old sweater and knit new socks or gloves with it. Father did repair work on the house and farm. This helped us to steer through those difficult lean times.

Chapter four
Political events

Politically Germany was in chaos. There were up to forty political parties, which shifted loyalties and names, and the government of the new Weimar Republic could not get many laws approved. Unemployment had grown to six million people. Chancellors resigned in short order or were assassinated. Two of the main parties, the communists and the national-socialists, fought street battles. This was a ripe field for a 'saviour' to arrive. And there was one in waiting. Adolf Hitler, a dynamic speaker, leader of the National Socialist German Workers Party. The NSDAP, known by its short form as Nazi Party, made many promises. Hitler said he would rewrite the Versailles treaty, give Germany its dignity back and give it its rightful place in Europe again. Many believed him to bring better times back, others, like some of the Prussian Nobility, thought give him a chance, it cannot get much worse. If he cannot fulfill what he promised we can get rid of him again. But that was a miscalculation.

In 1932 the National Socialist Party got the most seats in parliament and Hindenburg, the aging president, reluctantly appointed Hitler chancellor, according to the constitution. Slowly a new age began.

For us farmers Hitler fulfilled one of his promises. He introduced an agricultural reform. The state would take over the debt that farmers owed the loan companies and they only had to pay back to the government as much as they were able to pay. For those who were at the point of bankruptcy, their debt would be forgiven. Several of mother's relatives profited from this arrangement and could stay on their farms. The government would then deal with the loan companies, mainly banks whose managers were often Jews who had very likely to accept the losses.

As previously mentioned, unemployment was over six million at the end of the depression. After the new government came to power it decreased to two million and later there was even a labour shortages in some areas. As a result of this reduction the crime rate in Germany had gone down considerably and was one of the lowest in Europe. The low unemployment was partly due to the introduction of the '*Arbeitsdienst*', a compulsory work force for young men and later young women recruited to rebuild the infrastructure of the country after its destruction and neglect during the war. It was a kind of paramilitary organisation in which the draftees used spades instead of rifles. This solution took a number of young people from the unemployment list.

The government acted in a way true to its name 'Socialist *Workers* Party' to alleviate some housing crisis. It built a number of affordable housing settlements for workers, several of my relatives lived in them. The party offered cheap or free cultural and holiday provisions and cruises for workers through the '*Kraft durch Freude*' organisation. These arrangements won the favour of many people.

I think the economic situation in general in Europe

and elsewhere had improved and one cannot give Hitler all the credit for it.

Though Hitler was born and spent his formative years in Austria, he said he was 'in love' with Germany. He had volunteered for the German army in World War I and moved later from Vienna to Munich. He became a German citizen at age forty-three.

But there was another side of the coin in the Nazi government actions and ideology which soon became apparent and which we could not understand. Hitler's racism, his hatred of Jews and communists and the way he treated them. He also considered all 'Non-Aryan' people to be an inferior race.

There were no Jewish people living in our village and the surrounding ones, and we did not know any Jewish students in public or high school who were abused. We did not see personally any atrocities done to Jewish citizen and had no specific information about what happened in concentration camps. I saw, however, the outcome of the *Kristallnacht* (Night of broken glass) disaster in our city, the demolition of selected Jewish stores and houses and the burning of their synagogues. Many of our citizens were appalled about these Nazi atrocities. I was abhorred to see what the Sturmabteilung, the SA, a German Nazi paramilitary force, had done to their fellow citizens and distanced myself from them.

The Nazis gained more and more control of the private life of our society, perhaps not to the degree of abuse of their citizens as in the Soviet Union. We could travel where we wanted to go, could congregate in churches and family gatherings as long as these were not openly directed against the government. We could go to our church without interference until the end of the war. Regulations became stricter toward the end of the war.

But we had to be careful with whom we could share our displeasure with certain government actions. People who did not like you could denounce you and the police would come at night to interrogate and perhaps arrest you and send you into a concentration camp

My father-in-law was a Mennonite pastor. During the war he was asked to pastor four other small congregations whose pastors were drafted. He noticed sometimes Nazi spies in his services checking if he would say anything against the *'Führer'*. He was aware of that. He would preach about the restrictions and the injustice and abuses of king Ahab of Israel and some of his people in the congregation would know whom he meant. But if he would have used "Adolf" instead of "Ahab" he would have been arrested and the congregations would be without a pastor, so he was careful with his choice of words and how he presented his message.

My parents knew the scripture that talks about the relationship of people to their government: 'Obey civil authorities that are appointed by God'. My mother tried to follow these rules throughout her life carefully, sometimes hesitantly, as far as her conscience would allow it.

There were two authorities in villages and towns during the later Nazi government time, the mayor who took care of the business like taxes and schools and the

Ortsgruppenleiter, the political leader who dove more into our social life and our beliefs. He organised the celebration of political holidays and meetings, following certain party rules and promoting to all citizens the Nazi ideology. How this was done depended very much on the regional leader. Usually the teachers were Ortsgruppenleiter. Our public school teacher had to be a party member in order to be allowed to teach but he was a low key Nazi. He organized sports events where students and parents participated. Christmas we celebrated as a community event together in the dance hall of the Gasthaus. We sang the common Christmas carols which my father accompanied on the violin and my older sister on the piano. Children recited poems and received small Christmas gifts, similar the way we celebrated on a smaller scale in the family. It changed somewhat later on and my parents withdrew their participation.

My cousin Eva's Ortsgruppenleiter was much more forceful to follow and impose party rules, 'to please the Führer'.

My parents wanted to obey scripture but also follow their conscience. A government that was discriminating against other people because of their race or belief, persecuted them unjustly and even killed them could not be of God. They did not openly oppose government actions but they did not participate in any of their party functions, except perhaps collecting warm closing for poor people and soldiers on the Russian front. They were passive resistant. Once my father spoke up against the party leadership. When the compulsory Hitler

Youth meetings were changed from Saturday to Sunday morning, he claimed we have freedom of religion in our country and on Sunday morning Church services are held which our family attends. So please excuse my son's absence from Sunday morning Hitler-Jugend or HJ meetings. For Hitler and the Hitler Youth, physical fitness was very important. I was good in sports, had won the bronze medal in a regional sports competition for which our group was very proud, so they did not say much to his complaint.

I think a number of people in Germany were passive resistant or indifferent. In our village were three active Nazis who would appear in SA uniform to party functions. One of them was our immediate neighbour. There may have been more sympathizers.

We had little intimate contact with this neighbour. Once he visited us and noticed that we had no picture of the 'Führer' in our house he reminded us that every German household had to have a picture of Hitler displayed. My father was not sure if this was a new law. He cut out a small picture of Hitler from the local newspaper, put a wooden frame around it and hung it on a sidewall of the foyer.

Our teacher knew that we were not in agreement with Nazi party ideology and many of their events, but he respected my parents.

When I had finished grade four in elementary school our teacher sent a letter to my parents suggesting to send me to high school, which started from grade five. High school was a separate continuation school for good students. They had to write a special entrance examination to be accepted and had to pay school fees. Since I was one of his best students he encouraged my parents to send me to high school. My father thought I should take over the farm and public school graduation would be sufficient for that. So he did not accept the offer.

At the end of the next school year the teacher, even knowing that we were not 'Nazis', invited my parents to the school and made the same offer more urgently. With a high school graduating certificate, the Abitur, he said, Helmut will have the opportunity to go to university. My father was at that time already suffering from severe depression and could not make decisions easily. So my mother took over. She thought this offer sounded promising for her son and would give him more choices in life and she could persuade my father to accept it. Before the new school year started she drove with me, the eleven year old, to the city to register me for the entrance examination. I wrote it and passed it. Mother spoke afterwards with the principal and achieved to get a scholarship for me, so that we did not have to pay the fees. Dr. Sahner, the principal, had been Consul in South Africa before. He was an open-minded official and did not ask about our political conviction.

After Easter 1939 I drove every school day four kilometers on my bike to the train station in Grunau, took the train to Marienburg and walked another twenty five minutes to the Winrich von Kniprode High School. That was a long trip and in late fall and winter especially stressful when I had to push my bike through the mud of the dirt driveway or the snow.

My mother wondered if there was a better way for me to get to school. She contacted the school authorities, talked to Dr. Sahner again and obtained a scholarship for me for the boarding school. That eliminated my long journeys to and from school in rain and snow.

CHAPTER FIVE
FATHERS DEATH

My father's health deteriorated. Bouts of malaria, which he had suffered in Romania during World War I, came back again. He had very high fever and bad headaches which affected his eyesight. We feared he would not survive. Once he told mother it might be better for her if he would not be around anymore. He said that once to me as well, putting his hand caressingly on my head. I did not know how to take that. I loved him, he had been a good father to me and I needed him but I had never said that to him.

On the 25th of July 1939 mother got the sad news that my father had died. He had gone to the Grüne Aue at night and had shot himself. Tante Lenchen had found him in the morning lying dead in her garden. He wanted to save us this tragedy happening in our house and being eyewitnesses of his desperate action, to take his own life. Even at this stage of his health he was very considerate.

Mother's siblings in the Grüne Aue took over the preparation for his funeral.

At that time suicide was considered almost a crime. Some congregations did not allow members who had committed suicide to be buried in their church cemetery. Members of our congregation were respectful and compassionate. Elders visited my mother and consoled her, offering help where needed, so did some of our neighbours. For me as a thirteen-year-old, this was difficult to grasp. I could not make out why this had happened. I did not know what a depression was, why father had done this. I ruminated on his action, could I have averted that? I had some guilt feelings. Perhaps if I had told him that I love him and need him and that I can learn much from him, he might still be alive. I can imagine my mother having felt the same way. She may have not tried enough to understand him and be aware of the severity of his inner struggles because of her positive attitude. At that time we had no words for 'Post Traumatic Stress Disorder', which may have lingered in father from his experiences in the last world war and now he may have feared the impending war again. He had sought help from counsellors including my later father-in-law, pastor Hugo Scheffler. Unfortunately he died before I found out about that, so I could not ask him anymore about what my father may have confessed to him.

After the funeral the family sat together to decide how to go on. We all wanted to work together to keep the farm running. My mother knew farming from her childhood on and had worked with father together on our farm for eighteen years, she knew what to do. My oldest sister had finished commerce school and was free, my other sister had just graduated from public school and I still attended boarding school in the city and was only home on the weekends. I was now the only man left in the family and I imagined I had now to carry the responsibility for the farm, a boy at the age of thirteen.

My mother was wise and sensitive. When she had to make decisions what had to be done on the farm she sometimes would draw me in, to discuss details with me, to give me a feeling of shared responsibility, perhaps she even valued and considered my input.

The economy had improved in time. At the end of the depression dairy farmers were paid six cents for delivering one litre of milk, now it had gotten up to twenty-six cents. Life had become easier for farmers; they could invest again in equipment and life stock to improve productivity.

Mother was caring for her livestock and treated it well, like companions. The cows had individual names. In summer, when it was milking time, mother would drive out to the meadow where the cows were peacefully grazing and would call them by name. When a cow heard her name called she would come to the place where mother was waiting to milk her. When a young cow was due with a calf and had difficulty calving, she would assist with the delivery, she would be a cow midwife.

She was gentle with animals as she was with human beings.

After we had worked together as a family without father for a year, mother could hire a farm worker to free my oldest sister, Magdalena, to prepare for work as a secretary.

Hitler had started the dreaded war, which we had hoped could be avoided. German soldiers had marched into Poland not far from where we lived. We could hear the thunder of the artillery. Bombers flew over our houses and we felt the explosion of the bombs they dropped on Polish military installations.

Magdalena had gotten work as a secretary at the

airport. When she saw the wounded soldiers coming back from the front, she felt pity for them and she volunteered to become a Red Cross nurse. Christa, my second sister, was drafted to the Arbeitsdienst and when she had finished her compulsory half year service, she was trained to be a telephone operator in a military airport in Usedom, close to the laboratory where the first long-range rockets, the V1 and V2 were designed. Mother saw her girls leave and accompanied them in her thoughts and prayers. In 1944 I was drafted to the army and fought on the Russian front. I experienced the end of the war in a military hospital recovering from a head and shoulder wound. I had the fortune to be treated by my own sister who happened to work in the same hospital. All three of us children were involved in the war efforts and mother was left alone on the farm with the Polish farm worker.

Through grandfather's connections she learned to know Frau Gehrman, the wife of a Baptist minister. Frau Gehrmann could not get along with her husband when they lived together for a while. So they separated for a period of time. He lived in West Germany and she moved in with my mother and visited her husband occasionally. She was a noble women and a very good companion for my mother. She could give her often good advice. Mother had also taken in a 'bombed out' retired engineer couple from Berlin and at times their daughter and granddaughter as houseguests.

When the war came to an end we soldiers made bets which enemy army would come into our hospital first, the American or the Russian. We were somewhat relieved when three American soldiers pushed the door into our hospital room open and pointed their guns at us asking: you have weapon, camera, watch?

After one month the Americans were exchanged for Brits when West Germany was divided into Occupation Zones, and for Russians, when the Allied Control Council divided Berlin into four zones and assigned each occupying force one slice of Berlin. Now a Russian soldier guarded the door and kept us prisoners in our hospital.

Christa had phoned us that her airport unit was dissolved and that she would join my sister and me in our hospital. She never arrived and we could not find out what happened to her.

We had no idea where mother would be. We heard that many West- and East Prussian people had fled from the Russian Army but we did not know if mother would be among those, if she might have been killed or even landed in a Siberian labour camp.

CHAPTER SIX
SEARCHING FOR MOTHER

The British agreed to transfer our hospital to Hamburg in the British occupied Zone. I now had to choose should I go with my sister to a more secure place in Hamburg or venture into insecure territory, into no-mans-land, occupied by the Russian army, to search for my mother. When I sat with my sister in her staff room praying for wisdom to find the right solution, it was as if I heard a voice saying: '*Your mother needs you*', that confirmed my decision to venture out on a dangerous journey into Soviet occupied territory. With a heavy heart I said good-bye to my sister, not knowing if I would ever see her again.

Hitchhiking on passenger trains, freight trains and trucks and marching many kilometers, I finally reached my home village, Alt-Rosengart, the first place I thought I might find my mother. Travelling on forbidden trains without a ticket was dangerous. I was interrogated, threatened, willingly mislead, pushed around and sworn at, arrested but managed to slip out again, even shot at. These were the most 'adventurous' seven-hundred-fifty kilometers I have ever travelled. The last part was a long march.

The narrow wooden footbridge over the small river, over which I had gone with my grandfather often, which would have provided a shortcut to our farm, had collapsed. I had to walk the long way along the river embankment to the main road with a solid bridge that was still passable.

Crossing it and following the road home, I came to our driveway, just behind the estate of our mayor Peters. When I entered it, I suddenly stepped into water. Meadows and fields in this area of the Marienburg lowlands were over a meter below sea level and were flooded during rainy seasons. To make the fertile land cultivatable it was drained through a network of draining canals. Pumps, which were built at certain intervals on the embankment of the river, pumped the floodwater from the canals into the river. The early pumps were operated by wind power, now they were electrically run. Since there was no electricity anymore available, the area was flooded and I had to step through water that would reach up to my chest. All our houses in this area were built on little hills which were above sea level so that our houses were on dry ground. When I stepped out of the water again, walking towards our house, my heart was beating. Slowly I walked around the house to the window where the bedroom of my mother had been. It was now midnight, August first, nineteen hundred forty-five. I took courage and knocked at the window. No answer. I waited a short while and knocked again a little louder, no answer. Somewhat disheartened I thought: What if my mother is not here, would all the trouble I have gone through have been in vain? After the third knock a quivering woman's voice asked: "Who is there?". That was not my mother's voice. I answered: "Do not be afraid, I am the son of Mrs. Lemke". Quiet for a while again. Then she called: "Frau Lemke, your son is here." I was much relieved and glad when i heard that. My mother was here. My trip was rewarded. God had guided my way. I walked to the front door and waited somewhat anxiously, wondering whose voice might have responded to my knocking. I heard mother's steps coming towards the door, turning the key and opening it. There was my mother. I hardly recognised her. She looked so small and thin. Her hair must have fallen out and was now growing back again. She was just recovering from a severe typhoid fever and was still quite weak. Tears came to our eyes when I took her in my arms. I had not seen her for a year. Quietly we went upstairs to our bedrooms. Mother gave me some bed linens and I made the bed in which I had slept years before. I woke up shortly before lunch. It had felt good sleeping in a bed again, better then on the hard wooden benches in the trains.

Mother served lunch, roasted potatoes and a glass of water. When I looked at her again in daylight and at the lunch she had served me, I knew I had heard right: Mother needed me to come to be with her and help her.

I asked mother to tell me what had happened during the year I had been in the army. She hesitated first but then started: "When the Allied forces closed in on Germany, people became afraid and anxious. They knew this was the end of the war in spite of Hitler's promise of his 'Wonder Weapon', which should bring us victory. We heard of the attacks by bombs and artillery of towns in the very neighbourhood. Rumours were spread about the atrocities of the Red Army when they entered East Prussian territory, especially the Nemmersdorf massacre. Russian soldiers had raped and shot women, some of them were found nailed to barn doors in cruciform position. A neutral commission from Switzerland and Sweden had confirmed that. Even several French and Belgian POWs had been shot. Stalin had given his soldiers free range to take revenge on the German population.

"Many people in East Prussia panicked and fled westwards. I had packed food, necessary items and valuables on the wagon ready to leave as well. We were, however, told by the authorities not to leave yet, the streets had to be left open for the German army to move back and forth. They would tell us when it was time to leave. They left and had 'forgotten' to notify us. On the 25th of January 1945 Russian soldiers unexpectedly came into my house. They pushed me to the wall and ransacked the house, searching for hidden German soldiers and other suspects and for food and valuables. They were the fighting round and did not stay long. The next round, the occupying force, was much worse. They raided the house again, emptied the wagon, which I had packed ready for the flight, and searched more thoroughly for food and other articles. These Russian soldiers molested and abused people, mainly women, especially when they were drunk and that was often.

Right after they had arrived, our next-door neighbour came to me crying: "Frau Lemke could you come over please, I am desperate and need your help, my girls want to commit suicide". Her husband had been drafted to the *Volkssturm* (peoples army)) and she was alone with her two girls, ages 15 and 18. I rushed over and talked to the girls. They told me, they had been gang raped by Russian soldiers and were terrified it could happen again and they could not endure that. They wanted to take their lives. I counselled them, I could understand their shock but life could still go on. I prayed with them for strength."

I asked mother how the Russians had treated her. She only told me one incident. "A drunken Russian soldier came one night into the house into my bedroom. He came to my bed, lifted my blanket and tumbled into my bed, I quickly slipped out on the other side before he could grab me and hid in the barn until he had left. I was always in danger.

"Our next-door neighbours thought it better to leave their house, which was like ours some distance away from the village, and move into an empty house in the middle of the village closer to other neighbours for better protection. They moved and I was left alone in our house somewhat isolated, about half a kilometer from the main village road.

"Frau Gehrman and my Berlin houseguests had left for Berlin in the last train that was going west. So I was alone on the farm.

"All my animals, cows, sheep, pigs, geese and chickens were butchered or trucked away to the Russian field kitchen or collection station.

These occupying troops were stationary and had taken over our farmhouses that made it easier for them to ransack our houses routinely.

"One day a Russian officer told me to get ready they will take me away. I had to go to the road, climb on their truck and they drove me to a large farm several villages away. There I saw the animals that they had driven away from our and surrounding farms. Not only animals, they had also gathered several women to work for them. I had to feed and milk the cows.

I worked together with Frau Lange and her two blind daughters and we became friends. After we had worked there for a few months the Russians were closing the operation and intended to drive the cows farther east, towards Russia. We were supposed to do the driving and may have ended up in Siberia. That was of course not what we were ready to do. We approached one of the older guards and told him that we could not go along with two blind girls. They cannot see to walk on their own and cannot work. He thought about it and told us the next morning: Disappear at night, I will find a replacement for you. He was still one of those rare, more compassionate older Russians. We left next night and went on a long march. I took Frau Lange with me home. She was the voice who answered your knocking." Frau Lange came out of her room and mother introduced her and her daughter Frieda to me. Hanna, the other daughter, was sick in bed, she had severe typhoid fever. There was no doctor or medicine available for Germans to treat her. She died the next day. I arranged the funeral for her. A few days later Frau Lange told mother: "Since your son is here to care for you and the food is too scarce for all of us, I will return to my home village again" and she thanked mother for being able to stay with her and left with Frieda early the next morning.

Our food supply was practically all gone. A few berries were left on bushes in the garden that were not under water and some fruit trees had still a few apples left. The Russians and Poles had taken all the food that was in the house while mother had been taken away. A few preserves stocked in the flooded basement which they had missed, mother had already used up.

Some neighbours had stayed and had hidden from the Russians or had fled, and the Russian soldiers had caught up with them and had forced them to return. They had been able to plant some potatoes on the neighbour's land that was not flooded. The potatoes were ready to be harvested now and the planters were willing to share the crop with us. Mother knew some edible weeds like dandelion, nettles, plantain that she used for salad to get the necessary vitamin C. The dried and roasted dandelion roots she used as a substitute for coffee. Even some perennial herbs had come back in the garden and mother could use them.

One main staple food mother had not had for a while was bread. I had seen a field of wheat that had not been harvested. Mother said it belonged to our relative, my aunt's father. The Russians had shot him and his son on his farm, presuming they were capitalists, so he could not harvest it anymore.

One early morning at dawn I boarded our little boat and rowed over to that field.

The only way to get around from our house at this time was by watercraft. Mother had pulled the 'Brühtrog' into the water as a substitute for a boat. It was a very tipsy wooden box which we normally used when we butchered our pigs. To make it a little more stable I mounted an outrigger on each side, like skis. It made it much steadier. With a long pole I pushed it forward toward that wheat field. I climbed out of the boat with two big jute bags that we had used to carry potatoes and sneaked into the field. With a pair of scissors I cut off the fullest ears and filled both bags. I lugged them into the boat and staked home. With a flail I separated the kernels from the heads and poured them into the grinder. Father had bought it just before the war to grind grain and corn for the pigs and the cattle. It was meant to be operated by a motor but we had no electricity to run it so I put a flywheel on the axel and operated it by hand. It was heavy work. I sifted the ground wheat and we had now wheat bran for porridge and flour for bread and cake for a while.

As our main food we had potatoes, which we dug up, from the common field.

One day, we were again on the potato field, I dug the potatoes and mother and the two neighbour girls gathered them up. We were almost finished when we heard noises, shouting and banging of pots in the house on the street where our neighbours lived. We assumed another Russian hold-up. We were afraid, especially the girls, that they would find us and hid in the potato greens until it became quiet again. Mother ventured to go up to the house to inquire what had happened. We were right. Drunken Russian Soldiers wanted to know from the women where the girls were and when they did not reveal that, they beat them up terribly with kitchen utensils. But they had saved the girls.

I had not been home for long when the Polish militia

stopped me on the street. Polish people had infiltrated our villages. They had been expelled from their home in eastern Poland by the Russians and resettled in East and West Prussia pushing the German population out gradually. They ordered me to work for the mayor of our village. I had no choice. I was supposed to care for his cows, lead them out of the stable, herd them on the meadow for about eight hours a day, watching that nobody would steal them and lead them back to the stable. I got one liter milk for my eight-hour work.

Once the Russians caught me on the way to work and made me work for them. I got nothing from them only curses if I did not work well.

The future mayor had not come to our village yet. He lived in the neighbour village Grunau. There was the Polish police stationed which would provide some protection for him and his property. He was afraid the Russians would steal his cows from the meadow and would butcher them, if he lived in Alt-Rosengart. Russians and Poles could not get along very well.

On my way home one day I saw a white rabbit in the yard of the future mayor's home. I caught it and took it home, expecting to have a Sunday rabbit roast. That would have been the first meat dish for us. But the next day a marauding Russian gang came ransacking the farm. They found the rabbit cage, which I thought I had hidden well enough and took the rabbit with them. There went our rabbit roast. Mother had been ready to prepare a good meal for us and we had so much looked forward to enjoy it.

In the neighbour's yard I also found a marten trap. We had no martens on the flooded land but a flock of wild geese settled not very far from our house. I set the trap on a piece of tin foil in the area where they gathered, to attract them. Shortly after I had skilfully set it up, I caught one. It had already died when I discovered it. Mother told me that goose must have suffered a lot before it died and I should not commit cruelty to animals. That was how my mother saw it. I did not put the trap out again. We had to continue to live vegetarian.

Once when I came home mother asked me: "Do you notice anything different in the living room?" I looked around, "The piano is missing". Mother told me, "I had been playing the piano, what I sometimes do when I feel lonely or melancholy, and suddenly noticed Russian soldiers standing under the window, listening. I stopped playing. They came in and asked me to play again. I played another hymn and they listened. When I stopped they started discussing something in Russian, which I did not understand and then picked up the heavy piano and carried it out. They wanted to send it to Russia to their family. It likely ended up along the tracks on a railway station somewhere deteriorating in the rain. I had seen that at other railway stations before, expensive grand pianos rotting and being used for firewood.

A few other funny things Russian soldiers did when they were confronted with western culture. One group had raided a house and one of them saw in the kitchen the woman cleaning dishes in water running out of the kitchen faucet. He found it amazing and wanted to unscrew the faucet to send it to Russia that his family would have running water as well.

One evening quite unexpectedly Annie arrived at our door. Annie was one of Tante Annchen's protégées. She had spent school holidays with us before and liked my mother. Tante Annchen had left her orphanage with all the other children before the Russians invaded. Annie had stayed behind. She did not want to leave. She was an individualist.

Shortly after she arrived, I got sick. I asked her if she wanted to take over my chores at the mayor's place? She agreed. I took her over to my boss and asked him if she could take over my work. That was fine with him. We did not want to miss the one liter of milk which I brought home.

My health was deteriorating. I got a high fever and diarrhea. Mother thought I would not survive. It took me two weeks under mother's care to slowly recover from typhoid fever.

One morning, I was feeling a little better again but was still in bed, I heard voices outside. I looked out of the window and saw three Russians, trying to reach with a pole, apples that I had left on the tree for later. They were successful to shake them off the tree and eat them. I thought no point saving anything during this time, either use it up or hide it well. I put my coat on and went downstairs to be with mother. The three Russians ransacked the house as usual. Since they did not find much anymore they cut open the feather beds to see if we had hidden anything in them and then left again, feathers flying all over the room. On their way out one of them looked back and discovered one of the basement windows which he had not noticed before. He returned and asked me what we had hidden in the basement. I told him it was flooded. He pushed me in, I splashed in the water and he was satisfied. The other two had left already with the boat and we hoped he would follow them but he chose to leave in the opposite direction in spite of our protest.

Our house lies in open fields between two roads. We have two driveways, short dirt roads, one leads to the Grunauer Chausse leading to the village of Grunau, the other to the Thiensdorfer Chaussee, which leads to the village of Thiensdorf. We had adopted the French word chaussee for street or alley dating back to the immigration of French Huguenots to Prussia centuries ago. We had adopted some other French words as well.

The two Russians had left along the driveway to the Grunauer chaussee, the third one was drunk and stubbornly insisted to take the opposite driveway. None of our persuasion attempts could change his mind.

He had to walk through the water and mother had to direct him with hand signs because if he stepped aside into the ditch he could drown. We were quite concerned.

Finally we were glad to get rid of the three invaders. We were, however, startled when ten minutes later the two of them came back and shouted at us: "What have you done to our comrade, where is he?" We told them he took the other driveway and went in the opposite direction. They did not believe us and accused us of having killed him. We could not convince them no matter how hard we tried.

They then told me to stand against the wall and raise my hands while they were loading their guns. My mother pointed out to them again the way their comrade had gone and tried to persuade them to believe her that I was innocent. But it did not seem to matter to them. They pointed their guns at me and I was convinced that would be the end of my life. German lives did not count for much to the Russian forces at that time, any reason was good enough to kill.

I was not afraid; I had faced death many times on the front. I could tell mother if this is to be God's will for my life to end that way, so be it. I pray that God will save you and get you out of this predicament.

There stood my mother a few feet away from me, seeing that the Russian soldiers were going to kill me. What may have gone through her mind? Seeing her son who loved her so much that he risked his life to search for her in order to save and help her to survive and now he will have to pay with his life for doing that. Mother was stunned; she could not implore the Russians to save my life. She knew of the atrocities the Russians had committed to Germans, they might grow angry at her or may even laugh at her, so she did not say anything anymore but she surely would have implored God for my release.

Unexpectedly one of the soldiers took his gun down and pushed the others away. I wondered why they had not pulled the trigger. Was he perhaps reminded of his own mother, like the one who stood beside me or was he stunned by my calmness, no whimpering or cussing, thinking perhaps I might have told the truth. They started to argue with each other and then the first one told me in broken German: "We will check out what you said and if that is not true, if we don't find him, we will come back, shoot both of you and set your house on fire". Then they left again.

About an hour later we thought we heard someone calling a name in a muted voice on the far street. Somewhat anxiously we went to bed that night praying that they would find their comrade. We did not sleep much that night, anticipating that they might come back and do what they had threatened us to do. We just waited. A few days later neighbour Thiede told us: a drunken Russian soldier came to his place and demanded supper. While he was preparing something for him, he heard voices on the street calling a name. He wanted to get rid of his 'guest' and told him they are calling you. The soldier told him he should mind his business and serve him supper; but neighbour Thiede snuck out and piloted the two callers in. They recognized their lost comrade and took him away. We were now much relieved.

Annie seemed to like her new job and she said her masters were kind and appreciative of her work. She also helped in the kitchen. When Annie came from work that evening and did not find the boat at the place she had left it, she was worried and called us from the street, shouting our names and asking for the boat. The two Russians had taken it and where just returning. They scared her, raising their hands to their throat, they told her they had killed her father. Quite anxious she came running to the house and was glad to find us both alive.

We were running out of potatoes and wanted to gather new ones again. We asked the neighbours if we could dig out some more. They told us, quite concerned, that a Polish family had moved into farmer Grübnau's farm to which our potato field belonged. Mother had seen Mr. and Mrs. Grübnau galloping past our house in their sleigh, pulled by their fiery black Hanoveraner horse, just as the Russians entered his farm.

We were not allowed now to get the rest of our potatoes, our necessary winter staple food. He would shoot anybody who would trespass, the new owner threatened us. That was disheartening. How could we survive? This concerned many of us since we could not buy any groceries, no salt nor sugar, nothing anywhere. A few days later, when we rowed up to the street we found the houses of our neighbours empty. The remaining neighbours had left the village, fearing they could not survive the winter without food. They had not told us of their intensions. Mother was disappointed. Mother and I were now left alone in the village.

Shortly after this discovery the Polish militia visited us. They wanted me to come along to our next-door neighbour's house to search for his Nazi uniform. The Poles had found out that he had been a Nazi member. Mother did not trust them. She thought they would take me away and begged them to bring me back again. They told her they would. When we came to the house the militia men searched the lower floor, I went to the hay loft to look and came to a peep hole in the inside wall where I could look into the hidden attic room. There I saw, draped over a chair, the brown jacket with the swastika armband and the polished high black boots beside it, the typical Nazi SA uniform. They called me down when they had searched unsuccessfully and asked me if I had found anything. I did not tell them what I had seen. The militiamen took me home again and assured my mother she did not have to worry, they were honest people.

Annie had told her employer that she lived with her relatives on a farm. He asked her if she had seen any farm equipment around. She told him sure there would be some. The next day our future village mayor sent a German speaking man to us and he asked if we had a horse harness available. I led him to the stable and showed him the one that was left. He looked at it and said; "I pay you three hundred zloty for it." I had no idea how much a zloty was worth. Jokingly I said, "It is a very good harness." He looked at it again and said, "I give you four hundred." I was dumbfounded. Somebody offering to pay for a harness that he wanted? We were used to the Russian gangs who were grabbing or destroying what they saw or wanted. He took the harness and I added a line to it. I accepted the money and possessed now Polish zlotys and had to look for an opportunity to spend them. That opportunity came soon.

Chapter seven
Being expelled from our home

The Polish militia came again, quite officially they handed us a paper in Polish, which we could not read and explained to us that we have to leave our home and report to a labour camp in the city of Bromberg. We knew that was the former concentration camp (KZ) of the Nazi government. We had three days to pack what we wanted to take along. My mother said somewhat somberly, "I wish we could have left with the others but now we have no choice."

I replied, "No way, Mother, are we going voluntarily into a KZ. We will escape!" I spent my first Polish money to buy a train ticket to go to town. I went to our former city hall where now the Polish government was stationed and asked the responsible officer in the main office to write me an official document that would state that we have been forcibly removed from our home. I thought it might help us to get out more safely and would be helpful to perhaps apply for compensation later. He did not know exactly what I wanted and asked one of his colleagues what to do. He then typed out a document, put an official looking stamp on it and handed it to me. I did not know what he had written on it because I still did not know enough Polish but I folded it neatly, put it in my pocket and went home again. Mother had already packed a few things that the Russians had left, into a rucksack; I packed my articles in a bag. I sewed a dirty patch on a good down cover, which we had hidden, letting a few feathers stick out so that it looked old and torn and put it in a Jute bag which I had sewed from an old wheat sack. In that down duvet I rolled a can of homemade sugar beet syrup and a few photographs, which I had been able to salvage out of the snow into which the Russians had thrown all of our photo albums. To make it easier to transport our luggage to the station, I quickly built a small carriage from two bicycle wheels on which we packed rucksack and bags. I had found out at the railway station when the next train going west would leave and early in the morning we said good-bye to our beloved home.

We asked Annie if she would come with us and when she hesitated we tried to persuade her to leave with us, but she made up her mind to stay. She had a good job she claimed; she could live in the mayor's house and help in the household. So she stayed and we never heard from her again.

The night before we planned to leave we had another heavy frost and the ice was strong enough that we could walk on it. We had already noticed Polish youngsters sneak around the house trying to find something useful. It was time now for us to pull our cart across the ice and along the road to Grunau, the railway station. We hid behind a storeroom and unpacked, mother shouldered the rucksack, since I could not carry one because of my shoulder injury, and I took the bags. We left the carriage at the storeroom and entered the train from the other side of the tracks. In Marienburg, the next station, we had to change trains. Mother struggled with her heavy load along the subway. A young man followed her and with a knife he cut the straps of her rucksack and ran away with it before I could catch him. I thought, so what? It was actually too heavy to carry for her and the stuff that was in it was not worth much anyway. I told mother, it is much easier for you to walk now is it not? On the train to Danzig (Gdansk) the conductor wanted to see our train tickets. We did not have any. I showed him the document I had gotten from the government official. "That is no ticket" he mumbled but he let me go. The next conductor threatened us to throw us out if we do not have a ticket. He wanted a bribe, money. I did not give him any. One woman, who had no ticket and gave in to his threat, took off her sweater and gave it to him. When he approached a woman with a baby buggy who did not have a ticket either and could not give him a bribe, he pulled out the blanket from under the baby. I was appalled and wanted to snatch it away from him but mother warned me not to do it. In the next station an older man with a wooden leg and a cane came in whimpering, they are going to kill me. When I asked him what had happened he said: " A Polish guy wanted to take my bag and I hit him over the head with my cane and he cursed and threatened to kill me". Mother tried to calm him down, seeing that the fellow did not follow him and come into the train.

My former document did not do it anymore. The next conductor asked for my ticket and when I told him I did not have one and handed him the paper, he wanted to see my identification. I showed him my substitute passport; he looked at it, then took it and my paper away from me and put it in his folder. He did not give it back to me, hoping perhaps for a bribe later.

On every station another problem came up. A youngster came into the compartment, saw my bag, grabbed it and wanted to disappear with it. I had two bags tied together. I could carry them only on one shoulder because of my war injury. I held on to the other bag and he could not pull it out from me. He left cursing. The following station he came back with two militiamen. When he came into my compartment he pointed me out to them. The first one approached me, looked at me and gave me a blow with his rifle butt that I tumbled into the opposite wall. That was hurtful. As I was lying in the corner, he took the bags and gave them to the boy. Then he opened the jute bags saw the patched up down duvet and said snobbishly; "Old blanket, you can keep it." He asked for my identification. I had none; the conductor had not given it back to me. " I have to arrest you", he told me in a stern voice, "Come out!" When I was on the platform I saw my mother getting out as well. I told her to stay inside and travel on, it is easier for me to escape alone, but she did not want to lose me, she wanted to stay with me and help me if she could. The two militiamen were marching me off the platform, one ahead, the other behind me and mother following us. We passed the conductor who had my papers. He had his folder open conferring with a passenger. I told my guards this is the man who has my papers. I went up to him, took the folder from the surprised conductor, pulled out my identification and gave the folder back to him. I showed the papers to the militiaman, " documenta dobre?", I asked him. The train was starting to roll out, I quickly opened the door, helped mother in, then jumped into the moving train and closed the door behind me. The startled militiamen stood on the platform and saw the train and us disappear.

The closer we came to the East German border the more problematic things seemed to become. The railway officials were making it unreasonably difficult and awkward for us passengers. They stopped the train shortly before it came to the platform and expected us to disembark beside the open tracks. That made it almost impossible, especially for older people, handicapped and women with baby buggies to get out. Some passengers had to throw their luggage out first, jump or crawl down the steep step to the ground, then collect their luggage and carry it to the platform. This circumstance gave the Polish fellows an opportunity to 'help' passengers with their luggage, taking it and running away with it before the passengers had a chance to pick it up.

At the next station we were all asked to leave the train. All refugees were transferred into a freight train, twenty people into one boxcar. After the doors were sealed, the train drove through to the last station before the border. We had a ten-minute stop. Everybody had to get out again and people had a chance to hide behind the bushes beside the tracks to relieve themselves. That had become necessary for some of us. I walked around a little to stretch my legs and saw a small roll of heavy wire on the ground before me. I picked it up and put it in my pocket, not knowing why I did it. I did it just by instinct. The ten-minute stop was over and we were signalled to return to the train. When I went back to our boxcar I heard some raucous hubbub in the other cars, people crying for help. Some scoundrels had gotten into the cars and tried to take, forcefully away, luggage from passengers, knowing this was their last chance they had to enrich themselves. I checked if all the people that had been in our car were back, I counted them carefully and everybody was in. I closed the door and locked it. To make sure nobody could open it from the outside, I tied the sliding doors together with the wire I had picked up. As soon as I had done that, someone knocked at our door and shouted open the door. We did not respond. The knocks became louder, "Open immediately! Police!" Some of the fearful women begged us to open, "They will shoot us if we don't open!" A few more courageous young women said, "In order to shoot us, they first have to come in and we will not let them." The knocks sounded as if they came from rifle butts and threats became more serious. They even tried to pry the doors open. My mother, who is usually the 'follow orders' type said nothing, neither warning me or encouraging me. With the help of those fearless women using all our strength, we could keep the sliding doors together. Finally the train moved out and everybody applauded. We could keep the few luggage pieces we still had left and take them with us. After a short travel time the train crossed the Oder River, which was the border between the new Poland and East Germany. We were relatively safe now. The train went through to Berlin. All of us 'animals' were let out of the cattle car.

Chapter eight
Refugees

Very different from our experiences in the Polish stations, in Berlin Red Cross nurses welcomed us with a cup of coffee or tea and a slice of bread. They answered our questions and told us what to expect.

Those who had a place to go to, walked away or boarded connecting trains and moved on. Mother and I had no place to go. We knew that father's oldest brother, Onkel Gustav, lived in Lehnitz, a distant suburb of Berlin. But telephone lines were not connected yet, city trains and subways were not running, there was no way to get there. We did not even know if he was still alive and had survived all the heavy bombings of the city. When we went outside and looked from the station to the city we saw heaps of rubble. As far as we could see hardly any houses were left intact where people could live in. We were shocked to see such a total destruction.

There was no way for us to get in contact with Onkel Gustav's family. So we stood around or walked along the platform aimlessly until we heard an announcement: all the people who were expelled from Poland and had no place to go to were to report to the Red Cross centre. Quite a few people gathered there. We were given tickets for a train to Magdeburg, three hundred kilometers west. In Magdeburg we were registered, given some food vouchers and directed to a large former air raid bunker. We got a small room in it, two floors down below ground level. The only furniture in it was a wooden bench. Magdeburg was not as badly destroyed as Berlin, I found, when I walked around in the city. Mother did not feel so good and did not come along. With our food vouchers we bought something to eat. There was not much of a selection. We left our room in the bunker and went outside for a while to get some fresh air but it was cold outside and we had to go back in again to warm up. The nights were not something to look forward to in our bare dark room. Mother slept on the wooden bench. I unhinged the wooden entrance door and laid it on the floor as my mattress. I did not want to lie on the damp, musty concrete floor. We had no bed sheets or pillows. We were lucky that they had left us our down duvets which we used to lie on and cover us to keep warm. After having been three days in the bunker, I went to the authorities and told them my mother was getting sick, we could not stay any longer in this damp, sticky place. I was told that the city was putting together a list of refugees and they would be transferred into a refugee camp in Genthin. They promised to put us on that list.

We were back on the train again. When we disembarked and went out to the station square, we were greeted by a group of city officials, among them the mayor of the city, who welcomed us warmly and compassionately, acknowledging us as people who had suffered a lot, having lost homes and belongings. They would try to help us get settled again. As a token of welcome they gave each of us a slice of bread. We were very moved, we felt included, like normal citizens again. We were bussed to a Gasthof on the outskirts of town. In the large dance-hall of the inn sixty double decker beds had been put up, four together in a block with a meter and a half passageway in between, to house us hundred twenty refugees. I chose the bed beside the oil barrel stove. There was more open space in front of it. It widened out into a small sitting area with a table and a few chairs. Beside it, close to the entrance was the door to the sickroom. I had offered to heat the stove and keep the room warm or warmer than the outside. It was in the middle of winter. In one of these four bed groups, mother slept in the lower bed and I in the upper one. Beside me slept a young teacher and her mother in the lower bed. We all had to dress and undress in the same room. Of the hundred twenty occupants in the room there were only three men, one frail old man in his late seventies, one invalid with a wooden leg and I, still not quite recovered from my war injury. The others were women and children. The women had to help in the kitchen preparing the food and serving it. I volunteered to bring the potatoes from the cellar to the kitchen. Mother was not well enough to participate. We took turns in the small dining room. We had to get used to the crowded facilities and the noise, so everybody tried to be as cooperative and accommodating as possible. Mothers tried to occupy their children, which was not easy in those narrow spaces with no proper play areas. Some were creative and played simple games together.

One of the residents, a teacher, seeing all these children running around looking for something to do, reasoned under normal situations the children would be in school. Why could we not start school instruction for them here?

She discussed it with the mothers and they agreed. So all the school age children were gathered together and asked if they wanted to go to school again. Most of them were happy to have something meaningful to do. The teacher and some parents divided the children into age groups and classes and announced to them, 'school will start tomorrow'. Attendance was still voluntary. The owner of the place had organized a blackboard and the children exchanged pencils and paper and enjoyed being in school again. Some of the school age children had not been in school because of the war and were anxious to start it now. I had offered the teacher my help in organizing the classes keep discipline among the children and teach them the basic skills. This was my first practicum as a teacher.

I had an unusual student in my group. He could write the alphabet but wrote the words backwards and from right to left, in mirror script. I was baffled and wondered where he had learned that. To teach him to write the proper way I borrowed a mirror from a lady, held it against his writing and demonstrated to him the way we normally write. He was an intelligent boy and learned quickly to write correctly.

Mother was involved as much as she could. She got acquainted with women who were grieving and listened to their stories. Occasionally she helped women with many small children, by entertaining them for a short while in order to give their mother some rest. She visited women who were sick or lonely or sat with those who were brooding over the loss of their livelihood. Some of the young girls liked to talk to her and get her advice.

The invalid was sitting in a corner, weaving handbags and shopping bags with string and coloured wool. I watched him for a while and thought I can do that too. I asked the innkeeper for a small piece of plywood, made a template and started weaving bags. I showed them to mother for approval or suggestions for improvement. I gradually developed different styles and patterns. When we ran out of material, we went to town hoping to buy some more string but there was nothing available. I was able to get some remnants of coloured wool from a needlework store when I told them what I needed it for and gave them one of my bags, but that was all. We thought of other possibilities to get some cord. Perhaps a farmer who owned a binder-harvester might spare us some binder-string. On one farm the farmer's wife told us she just had heard that her husband had been killed in the war and she was now alone on the farm and did not quite know what we were looking for but she lead us into the barn and there we saw two rolls of binder string. She let us have them. We thanked her for it. We could now go on to weave more bags. Some of the better bags I traded in for things mother could use but could not buy.

My twentieth birthday was approaching and mother wanted to surprise me with a special celebration. I had traded in a bag for two loaves of bread from a woman whose three children were sick. They had not been able to eat their allotted portion of bread. The bread, we got shortly after the war, was baked with flour and a small addition of fine filtered sawdust and shredded red beet leaves, we were told. It did not keep fresh very long so she wanted to get rid of it before it got spoiled. I had requisitioned a few potatoes from the cellar and mother had planned a special lunch for my birthday party. Main dish potatoes roasted in the embers of the oven beside our bed, dessert, bread with butter, which I had traded in for my bags, and the last home-made West-Prussian sugar beet syrup we had still left over. Mother had invited a dozen girls to celebrate with me and we had a great time, singing and talking about the good old times.

A rumour went around, the camp was to be dissolved and its residents shipped across the border to West Germany. My mother heard that in the sick room. She had gotten ill with shingles, perhaps because of poor hygiene in the camp. The rumour became fact. All the residents of the camp were asked to pack their belongings and board the busses that would take them to the railway station. Mother and I could not go along since mother was still in quarantine. With a heavy heart I accompanied the people I had learned to know, some more intimately than others, to the station and waved good-bye to them and then returned to mother. The next day we two had to leave the camp. The ambulance took mother to the city hospital and I was sent to stay with a Genthin family. I visited my mother daily when I was allowed.

I was looking for a job to make money to buy food for us. The neighbour needed someone to split his logs to make firewood. I accepted the job and went to work at the neighbour's yard. I had split quite a bit and had stacked it up neatly to eye level when I spotted a Russian GPU secret policeman, recognizable by his green cap, going to the house in which I lived now. I got suspicious: What is he looking for? I watched when he came out again and I hid behind the woodpile until he was out of sight. When I came home after my day's work, the landlady told me, "The GPU man was looking for you. The Russians need workers to dismantle machinery from factories to transport it via rail to Russia and install it in their factories." Now she had to go and work for them. I shared that with mother and she too felt it was not safe here for me. She did not want to lose me, to be sent to Russia, not knowing if I would then ever come back again. So I disappeared for a few days and went to Schwerin, the city where I had spent several months in the military hospital until the air was clear again.

We decided now to go on our own to a safer place in West Germany. When mother was well enough we packed what we had collected in the meantime, bought train tickets at the Genthin station to the Friedland border camp, the official border crossing from East Germany to West Germany for the northern region. We got a cot in the camp. Next day we went to the checkpoint office to ask what procedures we would have to follow to get permission to cross the border. The first question was, do you have an address where you can go? We did not have one. The answer was: "We are sorry but you will not be permitted to go to West Germany without having a specific destition." Mother told them, "I have a brother who is supposed to live in a village called Hillerse". But we had no confirmation. "That is not good enough", he replied. We were sent from one office to another, always the same answer. One kind official had pity on us, he took me aside and whispered to me, "There is a man who takes people who are in your position illegally over the border, meet him at seven at the south gate." I thanked him. There was still hope and we had some experience in illegal border crossing. At seven sharp my mother and I were at the south gate with our few pieces of luggage. A man with a small handcart stood at the other side of the gate. I nodded to him and he nodded back. We went over and he packed our luggage on his cart. Six other people joined us. He wanted twelve Mark from each of us for his service. When he had collected his money he asked us to follow him. First we went through the outskirts of the city and then walked in single file along a narrow trail into the forest. Soon the trail petered out and we strode straight through the forest. None of us knew the man and we didn't know where he was going to take us, we just trusted him. After a while he stopped, put his finger on his lips and whispered: "We are crossing the border now, make no noises." Quietly we walked on until we came to a clearing. He halted: "We are in West Germany now."

We are relieved, we have made it, we are safe. We took our suitcases and bags from our guide's cart, thanked him for his dangerous job and he returned again, back into the forest.

Where are we going from here? No road, no houses no people to ask. We looked around and some distance away see a pickup truck under an oak tree. We walked towards it and there stands a Red Cross nurse beside the truck;

she greeted us kindly with "welcome to West Germany" and handed each one of us a cup of hot chocolate. We are overwhelmed. Mother asked her if she by chance knows of a village Hillerse and how we might get there. She said, "Yes that is not so far from here. You take the train to Hannover and the forth station is Leiferde. You get out in Leiferde and from there it is not very far to Hillerse. The railway station is about a thirty minute walk from here," and she showed us the way. We purchased the tickets, boarded the train and were anxiously watching the stations go by. We finally got out in Leiferde. The station was in the middle of nowhere, away from the village on a lonely road. Where is Hillerse and how would we get there? we wondered. We looked around and mother saw a horse and buggy standing a little away from the station. She went over to ask the driver where Hillerse is and how to get there. To her surprise she found out that the coachman was her brother, Richard. When she recognized him they hugged and tears came to their eyes. Onkel Richard had opened a horse and buggy taxi and took people from Hillerse and the surrounding villages to the station. He was now waiting if somebody wanted to go back. I put the suitcase and bags on the wagon and stroked Fanny, the little brown mare which I still remembered from the stable in Sparau. Onkel Richard had a number of questions to answer on the way home. He and his family had escaped the Russians just by the skin of their teeth. Like mother, they had packed their main belongings on three wagons, ready to leave. When the Russians entered the village they quickly harnessed the horses to the wagons and galloped out of their courtyard. A few times they barely escaped capture. For two months they traveled and lived in their wagons and emergency shelters until they were finely settled and registered in Hillerse. The army had confiscated some of their horses on the way, from the ones left he had exchanged one for a cow, had loaned some to local farmers, some were stolen and he had kept Fanny for his horse and buggy taxi. When we came closer to his village, he told us he would ask his landlord if we could dwell with them for the time being.

There was a great surprise in the Wiehler family when we drove into the courtyard of the Oelman cannery. Hugs, tears and laughter greeted us when we stepped out of the wagon. They carried our luggage into the house, we sat down and shared more news. After a good meal Onkel Richard introduced us to the Oelmans. Mr. Oelman, a tall, stately, middle-aged man, was somewhat reserved when he was asked if we could stay in the house for a short time until we found a place for ourselves. "If you can squeeze them into your quarters I don't mind". So we moved in with the family. The two parents had a room in the house and the nine children slept in the large room next to the cannery. They had strung lines from one wall to the other and hung blankets over them to subdivide the room into cubicles for the girls and the boys, the older and the younger ones. Now we had to string another line and hang another cover over it to create a cubicle for Tante Selma. But it was slightly roomier than in the refugee camp.

I was now desperately looking for work and there

was nothing available in the vicinity. I tried to help on the little farm Onkel Richard had started but there were enough hands in the family to do that. The Oelman cannery was not open in the winter, the girls hoped to get work there later. Liesel, the oldest one of the children, got a job as a housekeeper for a roofer family in Peine, a small town about twelve km from Hillerse. She asked her boss if he knew of someone who would have work for her cousin. A few days later she told me "I have work for you, the construction company, Hanke, needs workers for a new project". I borrowed a bicycle, drove to Peine, looked for the office of the construction company and introduced myself to Mr. Hanke. He looks me over, asks some questions and then shakes my hand and says, "I will hire you, can you start next week." I was tempted to give him a hug but bowed politely and thanked him for the offer. Back home again mother is exited for me, what she always is when I experience something good.

The next day we took the bus to Peine, went to city hall and looked for the citizenship office. The official inquired about the purpose of our coming and asked a number of questions. We told him we have heard when one can authenticate that one has found steady work in the area one is entitled to housing. He confirmed that and sends us to the housing department. The housing expert took our registration, looked in his list of available housing and wrote down an address in a village close to Peine. He gave us his note and told us; "There is a place in the village of Handorf about four km south of Peine which you can check out". It was too far to walk so we took the bus to

Handorf. The mayor, a friendly older man, explained to us the housing situation. A commission goes through all the houses and lists rooms that are not fully occupied and tells the owner he has to make them available for refugees. "There are about fourteen million refugees who had been expelled from their home in the eastern provinces and German settlements in East European countries and we in the West have to integrate them." A councillor who is in the mayor's office walked with us to the other end of the village to the house of the mason Rindfleisch. He was not very happy when he heard he has to give up one of his rooms. His wife, a hefty, talkative woman, tried to argue with the official but he said plainly, "it is the law." We in a way could understand their attitude and felt sorry for them. He unlocked the room on the first floor, on the left from the entrance door. It looked as if it was their living room, which they very likely only used when they had guests. They normally live in the family room beside the kitchen. This medium-size room will now be mother's and my living room, bedroom, dining room, kitchen and pantry. We had it sparsely furnished. A cot for mother, a small table with two chairs to be used as a workspace and for eating. I had a two-way piece of furniture, the lower part of an old dresser with a plywood lid to close it. We could store most of our few belongings in it. At night I laid a paillasse on it and it was my bed; when I had gotten up, we put a blanket over it and it was our sofa for guests if we had any. We also got a tiny woodstove for cooking. It was enough for now.

We had very little food left and were trying to get

some potatoes from one of the farmers. We knocked at the door of one of the biggest farms and asked the farmer if he could sell us some potatoes, we were refugees and had not gotten a new ration card. "We do not give anything to refugees", he said and closed the door on us. Mother was disappointed, not so much that we did not get any potatoes but about his attitude towards other people.

Later we heard that a great part of his stored big pile of potatoes had been damaged by frost and was rotting.

The next day we met an older widow from the church; she had heard the story and told us she has a big garden and had a good harvest of potatoes this year, she can give us some potatoes. When we asked about the cost, she said you refugees lost everything and do not have much money, you can have them.

Mr. Rindfleisch was very particular about his house. As a mason he had built it himself, brick by brick. He gave us strict rules what we could or could not do. Mother was always very careful and respected his orders. When she asked him if we were allowed to put some pictures on the wall, his reply was, " I don't want you to put any holes in or stickers on the walls". So we lived with blank walls. Once the wind from the open front door had blown our door shut a little noisily. Shortly after that he knocks at our door and reminds us in no uncertain terms: the door can be closed less forcefully. We learned to live with that and gradually got along reasonably well.

The village council offered to lease some land, a cleared part of the forest, to refugees for gardening. Mother was courageous enough to accept it. It meant we had to dig up the stumps flatten the land out and then plant whatever we wanted, potatoes and other vegetables to enrich our food supply. It was hard work but we were proud to have our own garden. On the way home from our garden we walked through the forest and collected some firewood. We borrowed a saw and sawed some of the bigger branches to oven size pieces. Responding to the beat of the saw, we were singing happily some folksongs and hymns in harmony. The stolid neighbours were standing at the fence listening to us singing and noting our unusual attitude to work.

There was no Mennonite church in the surrounding area. Mother went to the Lutheran pastor and asked if we, as Mennonites, could participate in their church activities. Pastor Brandes welcomed us heartily and his wife, a beautiful blond, outgoing person shook hands with us.

"This is what we normally do during the week" he explained. Sunday service at eleven o'clock in the church, Wednesday Bible study in the vestry and the prayer group meets on Friday in the parsonage. There is also a youth group meeting". Next Sunday we sat in a pew in a protestant church, listened to the sermon and sang the familiar songs with the congregation accompanied by the small pipe-organ.

We soon became friends with the young pastor couple. They recognized mother's gift of counselling, she could listen, try to understand and could give humble, unobtrusive advice. Girls and young women trusted her, confessed to her and sought her advice. The pastor included her in his pastoral ministrations and asked her if she would like to visit sick people or those who were lonely or had been abused.

Though we were refugees, who were by some still treated as second-rate citizen, mother was well respected in the community.

The housing commission went through homes again a few years later to look for unoccupied rooms that were needed for new refugees. They designated the upstairs room in the house we lived in for that purpose. The Rindfleischs had used that room only for a birthday party in summer. In order not to get a new person in his house, Mr. Rindfleisch told mother, "We will let you use the room. Your son can just sleep there, but he cannot use the rest of the room. He is not allowed to sit on the sofa". They threw a blanket over it and laid a coloured wool string across it to check if I had sat on it. I thought this was ridiculous. I took the string away when I sat on the sofa and put it back when I left. I also took my schoolwork up when I had to work late and did not want to disturb mother. The room could not be heated. One night during the extremely cold winter, when I had to write my final essay, it was so cold that the ink in my fountain pen froze. I had to scrape the ice off it with a knife to continue writing.

The pastor had also been approached and asked to make two rooms available. Mrs. Brandes came over and asked us if we would like to move into the parsonage. Mother was somewhat hesitant. "We are getting along with the Rindfleischs now fairly well, maybe we should stay here". I said, "Mother, the way they have been treating us was not very kind and they would throw us out if they could. We should accept the offer and get out of here. We are spending quite a bit of time in the parsonage anyway". I could convince mother and the fact that we would have two rooms was attractive. Two days later we said good-bye to the Rindfleischs, packed our belongings into a Wagon, which we had hired, and drove to the other end of the village to the parsonage. The Rindfleischs saw us leave with mixed feelings, happy that they had their house for themselves again, on the other hand the uncertainty who might come in next. And as we heard the next were a disaster. The new family that moved in, did not accept their restrictive house rules as calmly and humbly as mother did. They insisted on their rights and entitlement. Later when Mrs. Rindfleisch met mother in the store, she confessed to her: "Mrs. Lemke it was so nice when you lived with us".

Mother had the remarkable ability to adjust to different situations, like some animals can camouflage to have a better chance of survival.

Chapter nine
Handorf Parsonage

The parsonage was a tall half-timbered former farmhouse sitting on a big lot, adjacent to the church. The pastor would walk from the church down to a narrow footbridge leading over a small winding creek, open the crooked gate and walk along a path through an almost park-like garden to his living quarters on the bottom floor. Our rooms were on the first floor. From a short hall we entered into a big room with a brown, high tiled stove. In the back a door lead into a smaller room. This would be mother's bedroom. On one side of it we marked off a small kitchenette. The big room would be our living and dining room and for the night my bedroom. The windows faced the garden with a tall chestnut tree on the side of it. In spring it had those colourful, almost Christmas tree like flower buds, which made it appear somewhat majestic.

The pastor's family welcomed us heartily, quite different from the reception we received from the Oelmanns and Rindfleischs. They helped us with furniture. Mother could sleep in a comfortable bed again. Our living room was big enough for a bed sofa, a good size table with chairs that we could invite and entertain guests, and it had an old-fashioned tile stove, similar to the one we had back at home. We could heat it and regulate the temperature the way we liked it and it even gave us an opportunity to keep our food warm in the stove.

We asked the Brandes the same question as we had asked the Rindfleischs: if we could decorate our rooms by hanging pictures on walls. Their reply was: "This is not our house; you can do what you like". So we chose pictures and artistic posters, suitable for decorating each room. This gave our living area now a more homelike atmosphere.

Gerda Krüger, a young refugee woman with her two year old daughter, Dagmar, lived one floor above us. She had gotten news that her husband was missing from the Russian front and perhaps not alive anymore. She was sometimes in a depressive mood and was weeping. Mother was talking to her, encouraging her, trying to raise her hope. One day, very unexpectedly a man came to the parsonage asking if a Gerda Krüger was living here. He had been in a Russian prisoner of war camp for several years and had found his wife's present address through a person-search organisation. There he stood, pale and thin in a torn up uniform, asking for his wife. Gerda came rushing down and flew into his arms, weeping and laughing at the same time. Mother could feel with her, she had a similar experience when she saw me standing in front of her door at home. We all were celebrating with them. Mother has a winning way to join in compassionately when someone is in high spirits and celebrating.

Frau Brandes showed mother her big garden and told her, "it is almost too big for us to cultivate, I gladly give you a garden plot for yourself if you want that." Mother accepted it gladly and we planted potatoes, vegetables and herbs in our new garden. We gave up our plot on the cleared forestland on the outskirts of the village. It was not very fecund or high yielding, in spite of the chicken manure we had mixed into it. Perhaps it had not yet had enough sun to grow fertile bacteria.

Attached to the living quarters of the parsonage was a stable, which was mostly used for storage. Mother asked the pastor if we could keep some chicken in it and he had nothing against that. We got four hens and made a little chicken coop for them in one corner of the stable. We fenced in a small free run behind the stable to keep them healthy and happy. Now we could supplement our meals with fresh eggs from our own hens and enjoy an occasional chicken roast. We could get the feed free from farmer Brandes as a thank you gift for the work mother had been doing for him.

Farmer Brandes occasionally needed help on his farm especially during harvest time, mother stepped in, she did not only help bringing in the harvest, she could also give, from her experience as a farmer's daughter, tips how to improve agricultural practices. Brandes accepted and respected her wisdom and help.

I noticed mother becoming more alive again. She was freer in her own place, like she was on her farm at home. She did not feel henpecked by landlords anymore and agreed with me now that it had been a good idea to move to the parsonage.

I wanted to plan my future and thought the best thing I could do is to learn a trade. I thought about becoming a cabinetmaker and furniture designer, since I liked to work with wood. Mother supported me in that decision. I tried all the cabinetmakers in the area and furniture factories in the circumjacent towns; nobody wanted me as an apprentice. Either they did not have any work or I was too old. They feared they could not push me around that easily anymore as they could with fifteen year olds. I finally consulted the guild master for advice. He asked me what I had done before I was expelled from my home. I told him I had attended high school and was drafted to the army when I was in grade eleven. He suggested I should finish highschool, that would give me a chance to go to university later. I discussed that with mother and she encouraged me to do that, she would help me. We had just received the Lastenausgleich, financial compensation for property we had to give up to Poland. That money was not much but would keep us going for a while. I worked with mother at farmer Brandes occasionally to earn some extra cash.

I followed the guild-master's advice and applied at the Peiner Oberschule for admittance, was accepted and spent one year in a classroom. I think that year was good for my personal and social development. I had an exceptional homeroom and German teacher. He did not only teach his subject but also installed and confirmed in us social and spiritual values which I had neglected during those rough war years as a soldier and refugee where I had to struggle for survival.

I completed high school successfully and with my graduation, the abitur, met the requirement to enter university. Mother encouraged me to take the next step in my education and apply for university. It was not so easy to get accepted. Many university buildings had been destroyed during the war, a number of professors had been killed fighting in the war or were still in prisoner of war camps. After a few attempts at different universities I was accepted at the Technical University Braunschweig. I had half a year time before matriculation. Contractor Hanke had some work for me and the pay was good so I could save enough at least for the first semester. We had to be able to finance the first two semesters from our own resources before we could apply for a grant. Mother wanted to help me financially and took on work. She was going to polish floor tiles at a factory outlet close by. I did not approve of it because it was too strenuous for her but she insisted. After a few month she realised the work was too hard on her hands and since she was paid by the piece she did not make much money. So I could convince her to quit. After the second semester I saw a notice on the bulletin board: Free room for a needy student. I applied, the president of the university had made that offer. He asked me a few questions why I applied and then, when he found out that I was 'needy' told me I could move in. The maid would tell me when breakfast will be served. I was surprised and mother was happy that I could save two hours travel time each day and have a substantial free breakfast. The dinner in the Mensa was not very expensive and I made my own supper enriched with Mennonite Central Committee (MCC) canned food. That kept me going at the university.

After we had lived in the parsonage with the Brandes family for about seven years, Pastor Brandes was transferred to another town and a pastor's widow, Frau Lohman with her three young sons moved into the parsonage. She was an outgoing, compassionate and active woman. Mother developed a good relationship with her and her children. Her boys Christoph, Hans and Volker, loved mother and adopted her as their grandmother and I was their friend. Frau Lohman was a good pianist. Sometimes we would get together and sing hymns in harmony, which she would accompany on the piano.

Lohman family and Mother

After an MCC peace seminar for students the leader of the seminar asked me if I was interested in a scholarship for a Mennonite college in the USA. I gladly accepted and spent the next year in Bluffton College Ohio. Mother was well established in the parsonage, could live now on her government pension, had several friends in the village and was well engaged in church activities. She could easily let me go for a while.

America was a new experience for me. To be engulfed in a different culture was eye opening and widened my horizon. I learned to see and accept other ways of thinking. I made new friends, learned to know Afro-Americans and indigenous people and improved my school English.

When the two semesters were finished, I still had some time left before returning home to Germany and decided to travel through the USA, through all the different landscapes of this great country. In Washington

I stayed a few days at the home of Rev. Hugo and Susa Scheffler, recent immigrants from Germany. I got a little more closely acquainted with their daughter, Hildegard. When I came home I told mother about our relationship. She said, " I know the Schefflers, I sang with Susa in your dad's choir." Quietly she approved of our relationship but did not say much about it. She did not want to interfere in any way. When I finished university and got my degree as Diplom Ingenieur, I wanted to see Hildegard again. We had written to each other for three years and our relationship had developed and become quite intimate, so I considered immigrating to Canada. My sister had immigrated to Vancouver three years earlier, so I had a sponsor. I tried to persuade my mother to come with me but she said in her wisdom I should go first and when I was established she might come too. I could see her point. Her work in the church was appreciated and she had become a kind of surrogate mother, confessor and advisor for several nieces and girls. She did not want to leave yet. So I immigrated without mother.

CHAPTER TEN
CANADA

One week after my arrival in Vancouver, Hildegard and I got engaged and after she had finished university we got married. We missed mother very much at the wedding ceremony. We were sorry that she could not celebrate with us.

Two years later the political situation in Europe became quite insecure. The Cold War between Russia and America flared up. When the Russian tanks rolled into Czechoslovakia we did not know where they would stop and we thought it was getting too dangerous for mother to stay in Germany. She agreed and we sent her ship and train tickets to Vancouver and since she did not speak English, elaborate, detailed instructions she could show the immigration officer or conductor when they would ask questions and she could manage quite well.

Her Canadian family's lined up at the train station in Vancouver to await their beloved mother's and aunt's arrival. There was great joy when she stepped out of the train right into the arms of her children Magdalena and Helmut. We loaded her luggage into a pickup truck. There was one heavy box with a sticker, breakable, among her luggage. We packed it carefully into the trunk of my car and drove home with her in the front seat. She was very observant. She was amazed about the traffic. In Germany not that many people had cars shortly after the war, houses here were smaller and differently built. She had a number of questions about life and work of people in the city and was anxious to see how we had established ourselves.

Hildegard and I were curious to find out what was in that big box she had brought along for us with her luggage. When we unpacked it at home, we were very surprised. We unwrapped carefully a twelve-piece dishes set of Rosenthal porcelain with a platinum rim. With a smile she told us: "That is my belated wedding gift for you" and she enjoyed a big hug and thank you from both of us. We still value it very much and use it on special occasions in our home.

Mother with Gauer children

Magdalena and Gustav had just bought their own house, their family had grown to five and Magdalena could use some help. So mother moved first to live with their family. The three little boys were still shy when they saw the strange woman, speaking a different language sitting at the same table with them, though they had been prepared for their Oma's coming. That changed quickly when Oma took them on her lap and played with them.

Mother wanted to communicate with her grandchildren and enrolled in a night school course in English for Beginners. She had some difficulty to speak a language that had so many words with letters that were not sounded out, and its vowels had up to seven different sounds for the same letter, depending on their position in a word or their meaning. It did not make much sense to her. The phonetic German was so much easier to pronounce. The boys learned German easier than Oma English. But Oma's cheerful disposition and helpfulness bridged that language barrier.

She had learned and memorized some English vocabulary and sentences and used them proudly. Sometimes she even made up words that sounded right to her but did not make sense to others, neither in English nor in German. I remember one word, *Dressklahs,* for her meaning 'dress closet' or wardrobe and with a wink said: "didn't we say that in Germany also?"

Mother needed to be active, to have something worthwhile to do and she usually found something to spruce up, to repair, to arrange properly or set straight, basically to help where there was a need and a number of opportunities for that arose.

Mrs. Rogalski, from Magdalena's church, was looking for someone to care for her father who had a stroke and needed daily assistance. Mother agreed to help out. For the first month she went daily to his place to care for him and later off and on for a few months.

Mother's niece, Eva, had her first daughter. The birth procedure was extremely difficult for her, it had taken all the strength out of her and she did not have enough left to care for her baby and family properly. Her husband phoned in distress: "Tante Selma could you help?" So mother moved to their house, bathed the baby, prepared the food and helped to keep the house clean, work she had done and could do so well. Under Tante's care, Eva could gradually regain her strength again. The young family was grateful to have such an efficient aunt available.

Mother's 'fame' travelled around. When relatives and acquaintances had to be away or at work or were sick they could usually count on mother to step in and help out to do house-sitting or baby-sitting.

Hildegard, Mother, Helmut

When we had built our first house and started a family, mother moved in with us. She had her own room on the lower floor and could furnish it the way she wanted it. When Michael was born Hildegard appreciated her support. She adopted also a number of mother's recipes, and cooked meals, which I still remembered from my childhood, like *Flinsen and Saure Klops Suppe,* special crepes and sour meatball soup. We even got a small flour mill and ground rye to bake the healthy, solid mixed German rye bread, which mother had baked at home, a contrast to our soft, white wheat bread here.

When there was nothing to do in the house, mother would sit at the sewing machine to do some patchwork, darn socks or knit gloves or sweaters. But I think she rather liked to work in the garden and there was a good opportunity to do that. We had a fairly large building lot with a front and a back garden.

At the end of the street lived our neighbour Coffin, who had a big garden. One day we passed by her place and she called us in, showed us her garden, how her plants had grown together and crowded each other out, she had to thin them out and asked us if we wanted any plants before she throws them out. The next day we went over again with a big basket and mother came along to help to select suitable plants. Ethel Coffin is Jewish and when she heard mother speak German she tried her Yiddish on her. The two had fun communicating with each other, words they did not understand they guessed. Now when they happened to meet on the street you could hear them talking and laughing together. Yiddish is an old south

German dialect spoken in the Palatinate, where Hildegard came from.

Mother selected some of the flower plants for the front yard and the rest she planted in the back.

Mother and Lemke children

Our boys loved and had fun with their Oma. She was so amiable. She would play hockey with them on the patio or pull their cart around and chuck them out. In the evening she would take them on her lap and read them bedtime stories from a picture book in German, which made the kids eager to find out what those German words mean and they learned them.

Mother reading to Hanno

The neighbour next door, Mrs.Parford, had seen mother and had said Hi to her across the fence. Hesitantly she came over one day and asked if mother could perhaps watch her children for a couple of hours in the afternoon, when she was not home yet, she had to help her husband in his store downtown. She told mother she could take the children to school in the morning but when they came from school together with our children they would need some supervision until she could get back. Hildegard mentioned that mother could not speak English very well. But mother agreed, as usually, when she could help somebody out, she would do it. The three neighbour kids seemed to get along quite well with their new baby sitter, who would provide some snacks for them when they came in and watch that they started their homework. Mrs. Parford was quite pleased with that arrangement. She thought mother did a marvellous job. Once she said to us, "I admire your mother; she does things with the children, which I cannot achieve. When I come home everything is tidied up, the kids clothes are in the closet, the books, which they don't use, are on the shelf and the cups and plates are back in the cupboard; how does she wangle that, even with her language limitation?" She was just an amazing woman.

Mother and Hildegard

Mother was somewhat dependent on us in regards to accommodation and board and when she wanted to go to visit friends, she had to ask us to take her there or ask them to pick her up. When she wanted to share or talk with somebody, we were the only ones in the neighbourhood who spoke German, the language she was comfortable with. It seemed to us that she needed more space for herself, that she was not quite fulfilled and would perhaps like to be more independent. She had been her own boss most of her life, keeping the farm going after father had died, during the difficult post-war period, the immigration preparations and having her own household in the Handorf parsonage. She did not complain and seemed to be happy and content, but when we mentioned if she would rather like to live in her own apartment, she readily agreed. We looked for a suitable place in the Fraser District, at that time known as *Little Germany*. A number of German settlers and immigrants had concentrated in that area. Frau Wuttke, a fellow member from our church, mentioned to us that her neighbour, Minoski, had a suite for rent. We inspected it and found it satisfactory and affordable. So mother left our home and moved in to her own. The place was ideally located in the middle of 'Germantown'. Mother could walk to Sherbrook Mennonite Church, attend their German services, bible studies and woman's meetings. She could buy her groceries at Grimm's Delicatessen. Her family doctor Fast was a German Mennonite, also a clerk in the bank and one in the pharmacy spoke German; she did not need a translator anymore.

Mr. Minoski was a fisherman and often spent time on his fishing boat; during that period she had the house all for herself. When he came home from his catch, he would fill a bowl with herring for mother. We often profited from that as well.

After mother had moved into the Fraser-area and could live on her own again, she flourished. She had Frau Wuttke next door to talk to and ask questions where to get what when she needed it. She got more familiar with using public transportation and did not have to ask for rides to visit friends or go shopping downtown.

She loved visiting relatives in the country, the Fraser Valley district. She would go with them strawberry or blueberry picking in the field or just breathe country air again.

Mother, from berry picking

Since mother was living on her own now she had to provide for her life's necessities from her own resources. She had selected her *Lastenausgleich* to be paid to her as a life pension rather than a lump sum pay out. We thought it was safer that way. She had experienced several currency devaluations in her lifetime, especially one during the depression period, when a pound of butter was costing a million Mark. I still have a ten million Mark bill from that time as a memento. Her resources were her Canada old age pension with a guaranteed income supplement and her German pension. Added together it was sufficient to pay for her rent and her basic needs.

She had asked me to take care of her financial affairs, to make sure she got all her entitlements and benefits. She trusted me fully. Sometimes she would ask me how much she had in her account. When I told her, she would calculate for a moment and then say: " I don't think I need that much for my own, Michael is going to medical school he could surely need some money, write him a cheque". At Christmas she told her grandchildren, "I cannot buy you any gifts anymore, what I would love to do." Then she gave every grandchild an envelope with a bill in it in the amount she thought she could afford to give away at this time and said, "you can buy with it a gift that you like". Mother liked to celebrate with her children's families as on the picture below the families celebrating Christmas together with Mother.

Mother, Gauer and Lemke families

My mother was not a hoarder, she cared for herself well and wanted to be presentable, she did not want to be in anybody's debt. Her attitude towards money and possessions was simple: I need a certain amount of money to provide for the necessities of my life and what is beyond that I should share with others who are in need. When my mother died she had just enough in her account left to pay for her funeral.

On her way to church mother passed a house where she saw children playing in the yard. She was often attracted to children, so she stopped for a moment, watching them and listening to their play and she heard they were speaking German. She was happy to find another German family in the area. On her way back she passed the same house again and saw the lady of the house in the back yard calling the children. Mother waved to her and said 'Guten

Tag.' the lady looked up and went over to the lane to meet mother. After they had talked for a while, they found out where they came from and what they were doing, the Kneifels were recent immigrants from Germany. Ortrun invited mother to come in for lunch and she learned to know the rest of the family. As time went by they got more familiar with each other. Mother liked the family and introduced them to us. In time we became good friends with the Kneifels as well. Their children were about the same age as our children and they enjoyed each other's company. They trusted mother and when they were in dire need for a babysitter and their regular babysitter was not available they would ask mother if she could help out.

Mother at Krista's graduation

Not long after mother had moved to the Fraser district, she found again new activities to take on. Erwin, her nephew, was pastor of the newly established Sherbrook Mennonite Church. He asked mother if she would be willing and available to help him in his ministry to the church. He knew her competency to connect with people and thought she might be the right person to visit and talk to lonely or sick members in the congregation and wondered if mother would like to assist him in that work. Mother was willing and she visited those needy members, shared with them God's word and listened to their concerns, something she had done in the Lutheran church in Handorf before. Mother was good at listening and empathizing with people. Sometimes she tucked a small tape recorder into her purse and replayed the last Sunday's sermon for the persons she visited, who could not attend church anymore, and talked about an application of the sermon with them afterwards. She occasionally became the confidant to young couples, singles or girls. She also liked to visit relatives, the Cornelsens and Schowalters, who lived in that area and people from the German-Canadian cultural society. She would attend their meetings, and appreciated what they had to offer.

When we invited her to go with us for a concert or a special program in the German Edelweiss Club, she was looking forward to coming along. At that time there were still a number of German speaking churches in the area, other Mennonite, Baptist and Lutheran congregations. If they had a special speaker or topic, she would attend their services. There were more opportunities to get involved in this part of the city.

The Mennonite Senior Citizens society wanted to care more for their Mennonite seniors and built the Menno Court, a housing project with a number of comfortable apartments. They consisted usually of one big room with a built in kitchenette and a spacious bathroom. It had a washbasin built into a counter, a toilet and a bathtub with showerhead and grab bars. Mother was the first one to select her apartment. She chose the one with a view of the sports field. She wanted to see children playing and interacting. We helped her to furnish it. Gustav, her son-in-law, built her a comfortable bed sofa that fitted well on the back wall; I built a side table to match it and a small storage cupboard for her books and writing utensils. We bought a table with four chairs and an easy chair. Mother was very happy with the arrangement.

It was comfortable and not over crowded. She liked it simple. This was an improvement to the Minoski apartment. Now mother was living with a number of same age people with whom she could communicate. She met them in the garden or the common room; they could share their life stories with each other or play games together. Speakers, itinerant evangelists or missionaries would come in and bring them up to date with what was happening in the world, Artists and musicians were occasionally invited, choirs would come to sing to and with them or one of the gifted pianists from the home would entertain her fellow residents with classical music in the common room.

Mother was surprised when an old acquaintance and distant relative, Hanna Bartel, moved into Menno Court. She knew her from her former home church. She was a little younger than mother. Hanna had been a kitchen chef in another seniors establishment before her retirement and knew what life in a seniors home was like. The two renewed their friendship. Hanna was adventuresome and outgoing, mother a good teammate and could fill in what Hanna left open. They were a good match and would often undertake activities together, even cook or eat together occasionally. The friendship with Hanna brought mother another benefit. Hanna had a car which she could park in the Menno Court garage where it was always available. It was more pleasant and easier for a senior to get to a place in a car than take public transportation and walk.

When summer approached they made plans to explore the country and find good resorts or beaches to spend a holiday. They packed their necessary stuff into the car and drove to Oregon or California; they visited relatives in Calgary and stopped for a few days in Banff National Park. We got a picture postcard from mother stamped *Cabo San Lucas, Mexico,* a town for which we had a time-share.

Magdalena had booked a holiday in Hawaii for the family, when Ingrid had to cancel at short notice; mother stepped in and went with them to spend a holiday in

Hawaii and she dared to swim in the ocean. I think she was in her mid eighties already.

Gustav, Magdalena, Mother

We noticed mother was slowing down a little and she mentioned that she was feeling weak at times. She had difficulty moving her cooking pots from her stove; they had become too heavy for her. Her hands were not strong enough anymore. She went to Dr. Fast, he examined her thoroughly and diagnosed the beginning of a slow moving Parkinson's disease. We were shocked. Mother had always been healthy and upbeat. We got this news shortly before mother's eighty sixth birthday. We as a family decided to celebrate this birthday in grand style, since we feared mother might not celebrate another birthday with us, after we heard the doctor's diagnosis. We reserved the common room in the Menno Court and invited all relatives and friends of mother who would fit into it. We set the table, mother's place decorated with flowers around her plate, as it was a ritual in our family. Several of the relatives would contribute to the food. We ordered a big decorated cake from the German pastry shop, from the Konditorei, and the party could begin.

There sat mother at the head of the table in her elegant attire. She was particular in regards to her appearance. Magdalena, a registered nurse, went shopping with her mother, the dresses had to fit properly and be colour coordinated, for her age more in neutral tones. Hat, coat and handbag should fit together. Her clothing did not need to be from the latest fashion, just simple and good quality and representable in public.

Mother thought she was created in God's image, beautifully enough and did not use any make-up. I don't think any lipstick had gone over her lips or rouge color her cheeks. She did not use beauty creams to hide her wrinkles, they gave her face character. One could read in it what she had gone through in her life, that it had not been all easy and pleasant. Her smile would compensate for the lack of false colour.

I had borrowed a video recorder from the school board and recorded the whole celebration for future generations to know how we honoured our mothers. After the meal was over the performances started. Erwin gave a short sermonette; the family sang some of mother's favourite hymns in four-part harmony. Mother always liked music especially if her children or grandchildren performed it. Mother enjoyed visits from her grandchildren. When it was time for gift giving she asked the grandchildren to play their favourite piano pieces for her as a gift. She would ask that at most birthdays when we celebrated together and there was a piano available. When the children had played for her she would praise the young pianists for their good performance and sometimes, when it was not that good, add;" well keep on practising." She even did this to her future granddaughter in-law, as Tannis remembers from one of her first visits with her.

She told the children about her last piano playing at home, right after the war. "When Russian soldiers had ransacked the house and I felt a little melancholy, I would sit at the piano and play some of the reassuring hymns to regain some joy and contentment back in life. When the Russian soldiers came one day, smashed dad's violin and took our piano away, that hit me hard." Music was part of mother's life.

The celebration of this birthday was a wonderful experience for the extended family and relatives. We thought it could be the last one but we celebrated many more. Her ninetieth birthday was another great experience.

Chapter eleven
The last years

At the time when mother found it difficult to care for her household and prepare her own meals, the Mennonite Seniors Citizens Society built an Intermediate Care Home in Richmond, the *Pinegrove Care Home*, and she found that would be the right place for her now. She would get her own room with washroom, no kitchenette anymore. Cleaning staff would clean her room regularly. She now could eat her meals in the common dining room in company with other residents. She no longer had to cook and clean the dishes. A doctor comes into the home routinely to look after those who do not feel well and nurses do the rounds daily. Mother is quite content, with the place change. She knows when it is time to move to the next stage in life.

The management provides entertainment, similar to that at Menno Court. Church groups or choirs come to sing with them or for them, travellers or speakers would share their experiences and doctors would tell them how to age healthily. That sounded perfect for mother. So we helped her again to move into the Pinegrove Care Home. Her room was a little smaller than the one in Menno Court but comfortable and she is grateful.

She has again same age companions whom she can visit, share with them and bring a little light into their lives. She is well liked and gets a number of visitors. When they bring her gifts she accepts them under one condition, that she can pass them on to somebody else if she cannot use them or needs them.

Ben's wife's parents imported special articles from Germany that are not easily available here, among them particular sweets and chocolates. When Ingrid visited mother she brought some of those tasty chocolates and marzipan sticks with her. Mother accepts them readily since she cannot go out and buy them herself anymore. She wanted to have some of those goodies ready when children visit her. She likes to offer little gifts to her visitors.

Her grandson Gerry and his wife had made it a habit to visit Maria's mother once a week and have supper with her. On their way they stopped at mother's place, occasionally they brought their children along and spent an hour with her. We visited mother often and had once in a while lunch with her in the dining room. The home allowed their residents to invite guests to share a meal with them in the dining room for a small payment. She introduced us to her friends and we learned more about the atmosphere of her new environment. She could not walk to her church anymore. Richmond is farther away from the Sherbrook Mennonite congregation and her former friends. She now is more socially active in the care home where she lives.

She told us at one of our visits, that her walking became more arduous and her movements got gradually slower and were not so steady any more. We are concerned about that and advise her to be careful and take it easy. Also at night, she said, she wakes up because her back is hurting badly, a result of lying too long in one position. The pain would go away when she changes her position in bed but she often cannot do this on her own anymore and has to ring the night nurse. Sometimes she had to ring her in intervals of two or three hours before she comes or she does not come at all. This was one of the rare occasions that I heard my mother complain.

Shortly after she had confessed to us that she has become more aware of the frailties that come with old age, the home notifies us that mother has fallen and broken her hip and had to be transferred to the Richmond hospital. Michael visited her and when he identified himself as an orthopaedic surgeon, is allowed to have a look at the X-rays. He saw that it was a simple clean break and discussing it with the doctor thought that the break would heal again.

When Hildegard and I got the news from the hospital, we were in a quandary. A young professor from Germany had applied at our art college for a teacher exchange. The college had nobody who was interested to respond and my friend, Fred, asked me if I would like to go. I thought about it. This might be a challenging venture and I agreed to take it on. Hildegard and I had made all the necessary preparations for the exchange with Germany and we were ready to leave in two weeks. We now sat down with mother and discussed the situation with her: shall we follow through with our plan, the teacher exchange with Germany, or shall we cancel it and stay here to be available when mother needs us. She did not think very long before her response: "You just go ahead with your plan and fulfill your contract. I have enough help here with Magdalena and your children". Mother wanted always the best for her children, she wanted them to experience life fully, try out new adventures and learn from them. There was no judgement in her response, no 'What about me?' question.

When it was time to leave, we say good-bye to mother with mixed feelings. She is in good spirits and gives us a hug and her blessing.

The family took good care of their mother and grandmother while we were away. Eva, her niece, was working at Pinegrove at that time as a nurse and looked into her room occasionally to see what mother's needs were. And kept her company for a little while.

Mother and Eva

Krista has a special relationship to her beloved grandmother. She visited her often in hospital. She pushed her out in her wheelchair into the park. Oma liked to be in the sun, in nature. She enjoys watching the swans paddling gracefully past her on the lake at the end of the park and she hears a flock of ducks chattering, diving and emerging again with some food in their beaks - in her memory she sees ducks swimming on the pond of her former home place, Sparau. Krista even pushed Oma down to the beach and the two had fun together. Mother once dared Krista to help her out of the wheelchair and lead her behind it and then she pushed it herself for a short distance and as a joke asked Krista to sit in it she will push her. She has a sense of humour and she never gives up.

Magdalena's daughter, Ingrid, does the same for her Tante Selma. She visits her, brings flowers and keeps her company.

Mother was in hospital again for a check up when we came back from Germany. We had changed our return time and skipped a short holiday we had planned in the cabin of my school friend in Spain, when we heard that she was in hospital again. I visited her after my return from Germany and she was happy to see me back. She had physiotherapy and was asked to practice walking again. Proudly she showed me what she can do already. She would link arms with me and we would walk once around the hall on the third floor. When we came back to her room, she paused for a moment and then asked with a smile could we walk one more round again? And we did.

Mother had to give up her room in Pinegrove while

she was in hospital, because she had not occupied it for two weeks. Now she is just ready to return again. On a sunny, warm day at the end of September, Eva invited us to her summer home in Yarrow for a cup of coffee and to taste her grapes in the garden that were just ripe. We took mother along in our car. After we had our coffee mother sits down in a lawn chair right beside the grape vines so that she can pick and eat. We enjoyed spending an afternoon in the open together with mother. She was looking forward to going back to Pinegrove again. When it was time to depart, Magdalena and Hildegard linked arms with mother and lead her to our car. They had almost reached the car when mother suddenly slumped down and lost consciousness. It looked like a serious heart attack. We phoned 911 and the ambulance came and tried to resuscitate her but they were not successful. They took mother to the closest hospital, which was Abbotsford. She was in a coma. I remembered somebody telling me, heart attack victims being at that age, and mother was ninety-three, are often in a coma for nine days before they die.

We wanted that someone would be with mother when she wakes up again so we arranged a twenty-four hour watch at her bed. I stayed in Abbotsford most of the time. At night I slept for an hour on the sofa in the lounge and then was at her bed again. Magdalena and Ralf, when he had time, would take over a shift. Mother had not been out of her coma, shown any life, any movement since the accident had happened and cannot eat anything. She lied peacefully in her bed. I told her stories, read her scripture and quietly sang her favoured songs to her, not knowing if she can take in anything. On the ninth day, my shift was almost over, it was twelve o'clock, Ralf was to come at one. Mother lied quietly in her bed as always and I thought it would very likely not be different in the next hour when Ralf would take over again. I could as well leave now and drive home for lunch. So I left. I had just arrived at home, when Ralf phoned: Oma has stopped breathing; the nurse said she died when nobody was with her. We did not know if she ever gained consciousness again or just moved quietly over into another world where she wanted to be.

We planned her funeral with the funeral director who arranged her transfer to the Vancouver funeral home, where people could take leave of her. The church was filled with people who knew and valued her, who wanted to participate in the celebration of her life in this final service. Quite a number of them expressed their sympathy and shared how much mother's kindness, understanding and helpfulness had affected their lives. All members of the Lemke and Gauer families gathered at her gravesite to take final leave from their beloved mother and grandmother.

Lemke and Gauer families at mother's grave

The life of a wonderful woman had ended. She was a remarkable woman indeed.

She had lived through many time periods in history and survived.

She was born at the end of the nineteenth century in Germany when it was still a monarchy and had Kaiser Wilhelm II as Emperor .

She experienced the First World War and saw her brother go to fight in it.

She lived through the terrible depression during the nineteen twenties.

She saw the rise and fall of the Third Reich under Hitler's dictatorship and endured the Second World War, mourning with many relatives who had lost loved ones fighting on the front or being killed by bombing attacks or having died of starvation.

She grieved the tragic death of her husband when she was forty-three and had to bring up three children as a single parent in those lean war and post war years.

She was expelled from her farm in West Prussia, losing all her belongings.

She fled to East- then West Germany and lived as a refugee in crowded refugee camps. She participated in the recovery of her home country and saw its slow return to normality.

Finally she followed her children and immigrated to Canada and spent her last 30 years happily with them, learning a new language and adapting to another culture. She never gave up. Her love for others was boundless. Her Christian faith gave her the strength to endure and to keep always a positive attitude.

We have a rich memory of our beloved mother and grandmother.

About the Author

Helmut Lemke was born in 1926 in West Prussia, Germany. He attended a boarding school from where he was drafted to fight on the Russian Front in the Second World War. After the war he undertook a dangerous trip into Russian occupied territory to search for his mother. They were expelled from their home and he fled with his mother to West Germany. He studied at the Technical University Braunschweig in Germany and in the USA and graduated with a degree of Diploma Engineer. He immigrated to Canada and worked there as an architect and art instructor. He married Hildegard and they had three children. Both parents were active in youth work and church activities. In his retirement he volunteered as a director for a social housing society. He has written several books.

CPSIA information can be obtained
at www.ICGtesting.com
Printed in the USA
BVHW032310070820
585835BV00001B/65

9 781728 367125